ST. ANDREWS
HOME OF GOLF

ST. ANDREWS
HOME OF GOLF

JAMES K. ROBERTSON

Revised by TOM JARRETT

MACDONALD PUBLISHERS

EDINBURGH

First Published 1967 (Revised 1974) by J. & G. Innes Ltd.

2nd edition © F. Robertson & T. Jarrett, 1984

Published by Macdonald Publishers (Edinburgh) Ltd.
Edgefield Road, Loanhead, Midlothian EH20 9SY

ISBN 0 86334 044 X

Cover design by Michael Bassi
Illustrations by J. Putter

Printed in Scotland by Macdonald Printers (Edinburgh) Ltd.

ACKNOWLEDGEMENTS

Without the encouragement and the active assistance of the community of St. Andrews this volume could not have been written. The difficulty was never lack of help or of information from numerous sources. It was of sifting and selection.

For the generous use afforded me of an extensive library and picture gallery, but, most of all, of an unrivalled fount of knowledge, I cannot express too deeply my indebtedness to Mr Laurie Auchterlonie, Hon. Professional of the R. and A.

I acknowledge, too, the debt to past historians, Robert Clark, whose "Golf: A Royal and Ancient Game" is a classic; to H. S. C. Everard's "History of the R. and A." and to Dr D. Hay Fleming for newspaper articles and other writings on St. Andrews.

I thank the following publishers for having given me permission to quote from volumes published by them: Messrs Dent, Browning's "History of Golf"; Messrs MacMillan, J. B. Salmond's "The Story of the R. & A."; Messrs Ernest Benn, "My Fifty Years at St. Andrews", by Andrew Kirkaldy; Messrs Punch, and Messrs D. C. Thomson, Dundee.

To the Librarian of the University Library of St. Andrews and his staff I owe thanks for putting material at my disposal and to the Royal and Ancient Golf Club for various courtesies afforded. St. Andrews Town Council, by their encouragement and support, were equally helpful.

Lastly the late Mr Robert Tyre Jones was more than ordinarily generous in the liberal use he allowed me of his book, "Golf Is My Game" to provide a foreword that could not have been more fitting and apt. For this kindly gesture, I am deeply grateful.

J. K. ROBERTSON

SOUTH STREET,
   ST. ANDREWS.

FOREWORD

The most important place in the evolution of golf is St. Andrews. This volume seeks to outline something of the unique part St. Andrews has played in shaping the game as it is today; something also of the philosophy of the pioneers that is reflected in the spirit of the game. Golf is the most high-principled and moral sport ever devised.

No truer champion of golf and its essential spirit has lived than Robert Tyre Jones, of Atlanta, U.S.A. I consider it a very great honour that, in the midst of an extremely full life, Bobby Jones, with his innate courtesy, gave me full permission to quote the following passages from his last book, *"Golf Is My Game"*, as a re-affirmation of the affinity that he held for St. Andrews . . . an affinity that was born, surely, of the fundamental philosophy of golf. He was abundantly assured of the affinity and affection that St. Andrews holds for him.

Accordingly, I quote:—

> "I have often heard it read and said that a man's life may pass through his mind in the space of seconds. I am prepared to believe that is entirely possible. When I first learned that the World Amateur Golf Team Championship was to be played in October, 1958, at St. Andrews, I determined that I would take advantage of this very good excuse to go back to St. Andrews. This, even before I was named the Captain of the American team. I simply felt that this might be my last opportunity to revisit the city and golf course that I love so well, and that I should by no means let this opportunity pass.

> "Shortly before I was to leave, I was asked if I would be willing to accept the Freedom of the City of St. Andrews while I was there . . . I was happy indeed to accept any gesture of hospitality which might be extended to me by St. Andrews . . . It seemed that the only American to have been accorded such an honour had been Dr. Benjamin Franklin, and that the list of six or eight persons who had been similarly honoured contained the names of some great figures in literary and political circles. It was by no means a thing to be taken lightly.

> ". . . I have never had any reason to take pride in my ability as a speaker . . . In my heart I felt a gnawing fear that I might get up before the audience and draw a complete blank.

". . . Although I was not satisfied with all I had written, I determined that I would stuff some notes in my pocket, just in case of emergency.

"The hall in which the ceremony was to take place was a very beautiful auditorium. Within the few seconds it took me to make my way to the lectern I found out how a man's life, or a great part of it, can flash through his mind in an instant. I knew in that instant that I had no need for the notes in my pocket. I knew that I would have no difficulty in finding things to say to the people of St. Andrews. I was happy that the members of the international teams and the delegates were there; but, after all, they were to me merely sympathetic witnesses. This re-union was mine with the people of St. Andrews, and it was to them that I intended to speak.

". . . I am not the least bit ashamed to admit that I was deeply moved by the ceremony — as much by the awareness of the depth and sincerity of my affection for these people as by their expressions to me . . . It was a wonderful experience to go about a town where people wave at you from doorways and windows, where strangers smile and greet you by name, often your first name, and where a simple and direct courtesy is the outstanding characteristic."

No city surely ever received a more moving tribute that when Bobby Jones said near the end of his address: —

"I could take out of my life everything except my experience at St. Andrews and I would still have a rich, full life."

No other sport, few other men, could have evoked so beautifully moving an occasion.

CONTENTS

LIST OF ILLUSTRATIONS

IN THE BEGINNING

IN the beginning were the Links.

So opens the history of St. Andrews, the little city in the Kingdom of Fife, Scotland, which is known wherever golf is played.

This Scottish seaside wasteland of heather, whin, grass and sand, is where it all began; the international absorption with a game that is, at the same time, one of the biggest businesses in the world. This fascinating, infuriating, this frustrating, absorbing game of golf.

All-absorbing the people of St. Andrews have always found it. As long ago as 1691 the historic, grey city was being described as the "Metropolis of Golfing."

> "Would you like to see a city given over,
> "Soul and body to a tyrannising game?"

These words, written by R. F. Murray, the St. Andrews student-poet from America, have been true since the first days of the history of the city and of golf. They were true when he wrote them in 1885. They were true almost 300 years earlier when the Town Church congregation were being chided for neglecting their duties to practise their beloved game. They are true today.

St. Andrews is the traditional Home of Golf, and a great deal more. Its streets contain some of the oldest buildings in Scotland. Its ruined cathedral recalls the days when St. Andrews really was a city, the ecclesiastical centre of Scotland. To expatriate Scots its name represents their country and their patron saint. The life of the true St. Andrean still centres on the golf links. There he encounters all his friends. He recognises them, long before he can make out their features, by their swing. A golf swing to them, is like a finger-print — no two are alike, and all have their own distinctive features.

Today the essential core of the Royal Burgh of St. Andrews is a survival from the Middle Ages, and an infinitely charming one. The rugged and commanding beauty of the sea surrounds three sides of the out-thrust peninsula, and from its cliffs a vividly clear atmosphere enhances a panorama for miles around, of golden beaches and snow-capped Highland hills in the northern distance.

A leisurely perambulation of the town reveals that St. Andrews is much more than just the Old Golf Course. It is a dynamic community with a high civic pride in the present as well as the past. The townspeople are forward-looking, but they take pride in their historic heritage and everywhere around is the evidence in carefully preserved and planned buildings whose architecture ranges from the early Middle Ages to the ultra-modern, through Greek, Georgian and Gothic. The shops vie with the best in the neighbouring large cities of Dundee and Edinburgh, linked by road bridges to the ancient Kingdom of Fife in whose crown St. Andrews is still the loveliest jewel.

Without its visible bonds with the distant past, Scotland and the world would be much the poorer. The streets, quiet and aseptically clean, have yet witnessed tortured martyrdom and savage bloodshed. They exist today as one of the oldest examples of studied town planning, diverging, like spokes of a wheel westwards from the ancient cathedral walls and the old priory, for centuries the hub of the community. Now mellowed ruins, these historic memorials stand defiantly poised on the eastmost tip of the rocky promontory that is St. Andrews, overlooking the turbulent North Sea. Nestling at the bottom of the cliffs is the old harbour, round which weather-bronzed fishermen and caddies one-time lived, now a seascape for modern flats.

Even the most ardent and single-minded golfer will feel the urge to take time off from the golf links to savour the atmosphere of history that clings to the town's narrow, mediaeval backwaters.

In size and population St. Andrews is tiny, although a city in status. But it contains more expansive and impressive buildings of notable architecture than many considerably larger cities. Its fame and prestige are world-wide. Learning is almost the sole occupation. The teachers and graduates of St. Andrews University have exported academic learning for 550 years. The professionals and club-makers of the golf shops have for nearly as long exported golf knowledge and skill to the world. To the vastly expanding brotherhood of the game, the Royal and Ancient Golf Club for over 200 years has offered a tactfully guiding hand.

For both exports the world owes much to St. Andrews, and has handsomely acknowledged the debt.

The origin of the little grey city is as obscure and lost in the ancient mists of time as its golf. Its records are among the oldest in Scotland, and while historians discard the legend of St. Regulus coming to its shores with the relics of Saint Andrew from Patras, they agree that certain relics of the Saint were brought to the city about the year 736. There is good reason to believe that a monastery was founded long before that, on the site of a pre-historic settlement. The oldest remains of any building within the town are the foundations of a Culdee Church traced out at the Kirkhill cliff edge. Nearby, within the Cathedral precincts stands a puzzle to antiquarians, St. Rule's Tower, whose age they cannot accurately assess, although the belief that it was built as early as the fourth century has been long discarded. They place it tentatively at a mere 800 years old. This mystery Tower, at a later date, was overshadowed by the magnificent adjacent Cathedral, founded about 1160 by Bishop Arnold and one-time pride of the Catholic Church in Scotland. It took 159 years to build and made St. Andrews the country's ecclesiastical capital.

Next in age, arose the grim walls of St. Andrews Castle to unfold quickly a story of war and bloodshed. Learning came to Scotland with the establishment of the nation's first university in St. Andrews in 1411 by Bishop Henry Wardlaw.

The city approached the pinnacle of its mediaeval glory when it was made a free and Royal Burgh about the middle of the 12th century. Around that time, the Priory which came to rival the Cathedral See in wealth, was founded, and the Abbey Wall that surrounded the Priory's ample precinct, survives today in well-preserved and aggressive arrogance.

Came the Protestant Reformation which was preceded in Catholic St. Andrews by some of the cruellest and most bloodthirsty times in the history of Scotland. A martyrdom of horrible death came to many. One, Patrick Hamilton, was led to the stake in front of the College Tower in North Street and there slowly burned to death. St. Andrews saw more revolting cruelties in the sacred name of religion than any other place in Scotland. Gentle George Wishart was burned in front of the Castle in 1545, watched by Cardinal Beaton.

Retribution, swift and terrible, followed when Beaton was slain as the Reformation, led by John Knox, who had preached fiercely in the town and district, swept the country. Beaton's body was spread-eagled from the very window from which he had watched Wishart die, and left to hang for all to see.

After the Reformation the Cathedral, where many of the martyrs had been tried and condemned to death, was stripped by the fanatical Reformers of its Catholic symbols and imagery. It fell into neglect and later into ruins. Many of its massive stones were 'borrowed' and today decorate more modern houses and buildings. With the Cathedral's decay, the glory of St. Andrews departed slowly but remorselessly until it reached its lowest ebb in the second half of the 18th century. The University shared in the decline, and extinction threatened the ancient, grey city.

A traditional pastime—golf—played the key part in its regeneration as a city. The revival was accelerated by the remarkable energy and vision of Sir Hugh Lyon Playfair, both as Provost (Mayor) of St. Andrews, and Captain of the Royal and Ancient Golf Club.

At the present day a larger and modern St. Andrews encloses the remnants of the old city, one of the most complete and best-preserved mediaeval townships in Britain. It contains, not merely historic ruins, but old wynds, houses and buildings whose lower flats are vaulted and whose age is reckoned in centuries. It possesses a flourishing university, the oldest in Scotland, with many ancient buildings and treasures, including a hall where the Scottish Parliament once met, yet it is involved in the midst of a plan of vigorous expansion. The brilliantly scarlet gowns of the men and women students give a picturesque and colourful contrast to the douce grey stonework all around.

Education at the early age finds St. Andrews in an advanced position, with new school buildings, including a comprehensive High School. One of the oldest schools for girls in Scotland, St. Leonards is modelled on the great English public schools for boys, and has over 400 girls, most of them housed in nine residences.

The city possessed too, a really unique theatre. Only 70 spectators could be seated in its tiny auditorium, and it was converted from an

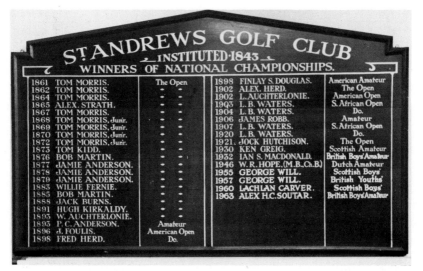

St. Andrews Club Honours Board

ST ANDREWS GOLF CLUB
INSTITUTED·1843
WINNERS OF NATIONAL CHAMPIONSHIPS.

Year	Winner	Championship	Year	Winner	Championship
1861	TOM MORRIS.	The Open	1898	FINLAY S. DOUGLAS.	American Amateur
1862	TOM MORRIS.	" "	1902	ALEX. HERD.	The Open
1864	TOM MORRIS.	" "	1902	L. AUCHTERLONIE.	American Open
1865	ALEX. STRATH.	" "	1905	L. B. WATERS.	S. African Open
1867	TOM MORRIS.	" "	1904	L. B. WATERS.	Do.
1868	TOM MORRIS, Junr.	" "	1906	JAMES ROBB.	Amateur
1869	TOM MORRIS, Junr.	" "	1907	L. B. WATERS.	S. African Open
1870	TOM MORRIS, Junr.	" "	1920	L. B. WATERS.	Do.
1872	TOM MORRIS, Junr.	" "	1921	JOCK HUTCHISON.	The Open
1873	TOM KIDD.	" "	1930	KEN GREIG.	Scottish Amateur
1876	BOB MARTIN.	" "	1932	IAN S. MACDONALD.	British Boys' Amateur
1877	JAMIE ANDERSON.	" "	1946	W. R. HOPE. (M.B.,Ch.B.)	Dutch Amateur
1878	JAMIE ANDERSON.	" "	1955	GEORGE WILL.	Scottish Boys'
1879	JAMIE ANDERSON.	" "	1957	GEORGE WILL.	British Youths'
1883	WILLIE FERNIE.	" "	1960	LACHLAN CARVER.	Scottish Boys'
1885	BOB MARTIN.	" "	1963	ALEX H.C. SOUTAR.	British Boys' Amateur
1888	JACK BURNS.	" "			
1891	HUGH KIRKALDY.	" "			
1893	W. AUCHTERLONIE.	" "			
1893	P. C. ANDERSON.	Amateur			
1896	J. FOULIS.	American Open			
1898	FRED HERD.	Do.			

First Open Belt, won outright by Young Tom

(Photo by permission of R. M. R. Morrison)

Last Fairway and historic Swilcan Bridge

(Photo by permission of R. M. R. Morrison)

Scene of Young Tom's tragic return

old Scottish byre or cowhouse. The theatre was run indefatigably and brilliantly by its founder, Mr A. B. Paterson, a native playwright and journalist. Appropriately, it was named simply 'The Byre Theatre.' In 1970 a modern theatre replaced it, built on the original site, but the new Theatre remains 'The Byre', and celebrated its Golden Jubilee in 1983.

Appropriately, too, and naturally, in St. Andrews a number of the streets bear historic names, while many of the others recall noted St. Andrews golfers. Visitors will find "Tom Morris Drive" — the 'Drive' is intentional — Sandy Herd Court, Auchterlonie Court, etc.

The oldest erection in constant use in the little city for many centuries is the Swilcan Bridge. It marked, over 800 years ago, the only pathway between the ecclesiastical stronghold and the town's harbour in the safe Eden estuary. It was the bridge over which traders brought their packs of goods into the town. The Swilcan Bridge was also the access from St. Andrews to its ancient Links — where the townspeople indulged in their own particular and traditional game known to them as golf or gowff. Practically every golfer of note since the game began has walked across it.

GOLF – WHEN?

ONE can only speculate on the exact origin of golf as a game. Robert Browning, in his comprehensive 'History' probably comes nearest to the truth in suggesting it is only one version of many ball-and-stick games that came into existence in Northern Europe as a primitive form of recreation. It is more nearly akin to Holland's Het Kolven than any of them. Another Scottish version of ball and stick is shinty, still played enthusiastically in the Highlands.

The development on the lines the world knows as golf arose from the eminent suitability of the seaside 'links' around Scotland's coast. The sandy soil, with its occasional springy turf and rare smooth and verdant surfaces, known as 'links' is interspersed with sand pits. Such ground was the natural proving place for men to discover who could hit a small, roundish object farthest with a suitably shaped stick. These components still add up to the finest conditions for the playing of golf.

What more natural, then, as in Het Kolven, for a target to be selected for this ball-and-stick recreation . . . a hole! In archery, and earlier still, in stone-throwing, a target was essential. The further development would follow at a later stage, of introducing the element of hazard that was a basic principle of early Scottish golf . . . the bunker or trap of the natural sandpit where the sheep huddled for shelter.

There could be more than whimsy in the explanation of Sir Walter Simpson in his "Art of Golf": –

> "A shepherd tending his sheep would chance upon a round pebble; he would strike it away, for it is inevitable that a man with a stick in his hand should aim a blow at any loose object lying in his path as that he should breathe . . . A shepherd feeding his sheep on the links, perhaps those of St. Andrews . . . rolled one of these stones into a rabbit scrape. 'Marry' he qouth, 'I could not do that if I tried' . . . a thought (as instinctive as ambition) which nerved him to the attempt."

The original harbour of St. Andrews was situated at some distance from the town, within the estuary of the little River Eden. To reach it from the ecclesiastical heart of the old city, the path lay straight across the Links of St. Andrews. That path is still a right-of-way to the mussel beds or 'scaups' in the estuary. The mussels were essential to the early fishermen of the town as bait for their lines.

So, there is significance that in those very early days, the Senzie Fair of St. Andrews, known to exist in the 12th century as one of the largest trading markets in Scotland, attracted goods and traders across the North Sea from the Netherlands, land of Het Kolven. The first Senzie Fair charter was granted by King Malcolm of Scotland in 1153, preceding the earliest recorded mention of golf by 300 years. The Netherland visitors would find the Links land between harbour and town ideal for their Het Kolven.

The circumstances were present and ripe, therefore, for the start of golf. More specific than that it is not possible to be.

In passing, the Lammas Fair, still held yearly on the main streets of the town, continues for two days every August the tradition that is age-old, of trading fairs or mediaeval super-markets.

Thus early, golf was started on its journey from the green Links of St. Andrews towards its monumental success story. For hundreds of years the game remained only a quaint national peculiarity.

Development came in three natural stages, namely, with the invention of each type of ball that could be made to fly that much farther than the last. The initial advance was the feather ball, or featherie, first made in 1618 in place of balls made either of roughly turned wood, or of flock. Came the big breakthrough of the gutta ball in 1848, and finally, the rubber-core ball in 1902.

Each successive improvement supplied added impetus to the fascination of the game. The fever of its spell spread first across the border to England, taken thither by James VI of Scotland as a royal and ancient game; then to the colonies, even to the penal settlements of Australia, and to the Western world. Now, to the Far East. Wherever the seed fell it germinated prolifically.

Today, golf is international. It is in the process of conquering the Far East. In recent years hundreds of courses have been built in

Japan where it is essentially a prestige game. Entrepreneur Zenya Hamada has captured the St. Andrews image by modelling his new course on the Old, and has also built his clubhouse on the plans of the original Royal and Ancient headquarters. He gifted £100,000 to the city of St. Andrews to be held in trust 'for the benefit of golf and of St. Andrews'. The third edition of this volume was translated for publication by him in Japan.

Its ever-widening horizons in the present century are locally reflected by the steady expansion in facilities that St. Andrews has provided to meet the demands of its growing flood of golfing visitors. Where for centuries one golf course sufficed, three more have been laid out since 1895. Another is in the process of development at Balgove.

In the 19th century, golf development was considered comparatively rapid when the Old Course of St. Andrews, home of the game, expanded in 1832 from nine holes, played out and back again, to 18 separate holes. This was followed by the layout of the New Course in 1895. But by 1912 still another course was found essential to meet the insatiable demand for golf, and the "Eden" Course was laid out. On this typical seaside course that is almost unfloodable, the biggest amateur tournament in Scotland has been played annually since 1919. The entry attracted ranges between 300 and 400 competitors from all over Britain, and some from overseas. The event, played in August, is regarded as a stepping-stone to amateur golf national recognition, and it has been won by many men who have subsequently gained the highest amateur and professional honours.

Within less than 20 years of the opening of the Eden Course, the cry went up for yet another in the town to combat the ever-increasing congestion. This resulted finally in the conversion of the Jubilee Course to a full 18-hole circuit of championship dimensions. It was laid out by Willie Auchterlonie, the last native-based Open Champion, and opened in 1946 as a full 18-hole circuit. St. Andrews, therefore, possesses four full-scale golf courses of top calibre and a nine hole beginners' course. All are municipally controlled. Concurrent with their development, the demand since the end of the war for Sunday golf has been reluctantly recognised by the local authorities and regular Sunday play is allowed on the Eden, New and

Jubilee. For the 'Old', enshrined in tradition, Sunday play only to conclude championships, if necessary, has been sanctioned, and was first exercised for the epic 1970 Open Championship replay between Jack Nicklaus and Doug Sanders, of U.S.A.

Extensive hotel facilities are an essential concomitant of the championship and tournament set-up; without them no golfing resort can prosper or even hope to compete. The tournament professional has come a long way since the days of Tom Morris and Andra Kirkaldy, and he, just as much as the hordes of holiday golfers and championship spectators, demands the best.

The fact that in the years since the war St. Andrews has housed at least one major championship or tournament every year, is the best possible proof that the city is well provided with ample hotel accommodation of the quality that is demanded. The British Railways Hotel which now overlooks the 'Old' is appropriately named the Old Course Hotel, and supplies a prime addition to their number. In 1982 it was acquired by Frank Sheridan, who has extended and converted it into the luxurious Old Course Golf and Country Club. It was officially opened in 1983 by H.R.H. Princess Anne.

This hotel, probably the most luxurious of its kind in Europe adjoins the famous 17th or Road Hole of the Old Course. It has replaced the 'Black Sheds', a rather challenging hazard which bolder golfers used as a short cut on the dog-legged fairway. It has always been the hope of Mr Sheridan that, some day, he would restore the outline of the Sheds which were used for the seasoning of timber used in golf club making, and as the depot for greenkeeping staff. Beyond the Sheds were a railway marshalling yard and a storage area for the local coal merchants.

FOR THE RECORD

CHAMPIONSHIP golf as it is today was first inaugurated in 1860. The Open Championship has been played on 22 occasions over the Old Course of St. Andrews, including the centenary celebration of the first-ever open golf championship to be held.

The Open Amateur Championship has been decided on the "Old" on 15 occasions, the last being in 1981. Four Ladies' "Opens" have been held, 1975 being the last time. The Scottish "Amateur", instituted as recently as 1922, has been fought seven times at St. Andrews, and the Scottish Ladies' six times. Numerous sponsored professional events have also had the Old Course as their venue. The "Alcan", biggest of its kind, had its inaugural run at St. Andrews in October, 1967.

The new Commonwealth Tournament and the Eisenhower World Trophy were both inaugurated on the Old Course of St. Andrews.

Walker Cup competition between Amateur golf in America and Britain was opened in the United States in 1922, and the first match in Britain took place at St. Andrews in the following year. Eight of the contests, in all, have been played at St. Andrews, including the two British wins in the series, the matches of 1938 and 1971.

Now to correct an international misconception.

The Old Course of St. Andrews is not the property of the Royal and Ancient Golf Club. It belonged to the citizens of St. Andrews and had done since time immemorial. It was part of their ancient heritage and had been in their legal possession since at least 1552, apart from a period in the 19th century when their birthright was sold in what was condemned as an illegal and disastrous transaction. A hundred years later the wrong was righted and the Links restored to the City. With the reorganisation of Scottish Local Government, the local control of the Links would have passed out of St. Andrews' hands into a wider Regional Committee. Accordingly, with the co-operation of the R. and A. the citizens successfully applied for a Parliamentary Order to form a Links Trust to retain local and R. and A. control.

In return for substantially helping to maintain the Old Course the Royal and Ancient Club has had certain playing privileges, and that is all. Nevertheless, St. Andrews owes a great part of its prestige, and much of its fame to the Club, although the R. and A. as it is familiarly known, was founded only comparatively recently in the golf history of St. Andrews . . . in 1754 to be exact.

Nor, during all that time was it the 'Royal and Ancient'. For the first 80 years of its existence it was known as the Society of St. Andrews Golfers.

The Old Course, on the other hand, has been in existence for the playing of golf since at least the early 12th century — some 800 years. More properly it could be named "The Oldest Course" because the circuit, roughly in the shape of a huge shepherd's crook, with its famous loop, remains the same today as it was in the beginning of golf.

The existing lay-out is the original and only lay-out.

Eighteen holes form a round of every standard golf course in the world, only because eighteen holes were played on the Old Course at the time that legislation of the game, by common consent, devolved on the R. and A. At one time, in the earlier days up to 1764 there were 22 holes on the Links.

In the same way as the standard round was established, every significant development in the game prior to the invention of the rubber-core ball is associated with St. Andrews.

A fact modern golfers will find staggering to accept is that, up to 1913, golf was free on the Old Course to all comers, inhabitants and visitors alike. The townspeople enjoyed free play up to as recently as 1946, along with certain preferential rights of play on the Old Course. Today, the charge they pay for playing over the four testing courses that now comprise the Links, including the 'Old', is still amongst the cheapest in the world.

While the sight may arouse envy in many golfing pilgrims, for the townspeople it is still unremarkable to observe the occasional clubmaker slip out from the shop at his lunch hour for a few holes over the historic course, to play over which has meant for some visitors journeys of thousands of miles.

Their seaside Links have, in fact, immemorially proved a valuable asset to the townspeople, although they have not always been recognised as such. Attempts at cultivation were futile because of the sterility of the sandy soil. Golf was being played when the city's most important and historic charter was drafted in 1552. Archbishop John Hamilton confirmed in it the right of the community to this ground and to play golf over it — a right that obviously, from the terms of the Charter, had existed for a long time before then.

The document reserves to the Provost and Town Council and townspeople the right of using the Links for "golfe, futeball, shuting and all games, as well as casting divots, gathering turfs", (to roof their houses), and "for the pasturing of their live-stock", the only type of agriculture that was remotely possible.

Subsequent manuscripts in the venerable University Library confirm this right. One, dated 1611, refers to the areas of the Links, known as the lands of Pilmure, the Links between the 'Mussil Scaup' to the 'Watter of Edin'; the North Haugh and the South Haugh; the lands of the Salt Grass, an acreage of links land much more considerable than the area taken up by the original Old Course.

These rights of the ancient burgh in the Links have been upheld and confirmed against all challenges, in the highest courts of law throughout the centuries, the right to play golf always being adjudged paramount. For more than 400 years any golfer in the world who cared 'to resort thither for that amusement' has enjoyed that legal right.

Archbishop Hamilton's historic 1552 charter has its own history. The document was lost for over 100 years but is again in the possession of its rightful owners, the citizens of St. Andrews only by sheer chance. An Edinburgh printer rescued it from the pulp mill in the last century by paying one shilling for it. He sold it to the University of St. Andrews for 45/-. In 1922 the University presented the parchment to the Town Council once more.

The University Court minutes of that date record that the Charter had been handed over to the Edinburgh law agents of the Town more than a century before, for production in one of the many lawsuits over the Links. The lawyers failed to return it. We quote the minute: — "It passed out of their custody and into the possession of a bookseller from whom it had been purchased by the University. The University Court agreed that the Charter be presented to the Town Council."

John Hamilton was the last archbishop of the Roman Church, the immediate successor of Cardinal Beaton. He was ruthless, even for those days. The ill-fated Mary, Queen of Scots (an occasional golfer who was criticised for playing so soon after the death of Darnley, her husband), was a captive in nearby Loch Leven Castle. Hamilton proposed she be put to death, "as the only certain method of reconciling all parties". (And, incidentally of advancing his own interests.) He himself came to a violent end and was hanged for complicity in the murder of the same Darnley.

Notwithstanding that the Charter was lost, St. Andrews Town Council remained always alive to their rights and did everything to preserve them. One was their annual custom of 'riding the marches', or boundaries, for many years as a public demonstration of their servitudes, or rights, including those of bleaching the housewives' washing on the Old Course, and of course, of playing golf.

The riding ceremony in 1851 was an unusually largely attended one. The St. Andrews Golf Club, whose members consist of artisans and shopkeepers of the city, asked permission to be officially represented in it. They wanted to demonstrate how deeply they were conscious of their rights as citizens in the golf links.

Just how long before 1552 golf existed as a consuming passion of St. Andreans will never be known. As early as 1457 the famous act of the Scottish Parliament that reveals the first reference in history to the game, had become law. It decreed that "The futeball and the golfe be utterly cryit doun". This was to compel the townspeople to devote more of their scant leisure time to the warlike practice of archery for defence against the constant menace of England.

The form that golf took derives much from archery. From at least 1618 an Archery Club competed annually for a silver arrow to which the winner appended a medal at his own expense. This club existed until 1751 when archery appears to have been superseded by the golf of the Royal and Ancient Golf Club in 1754. The R. and A. instituted a Silver Putter on which balls were and still are appended by the winner — a continuation of the old archery custom.

Records throughout the 16th century reveal that the Church was just as much concerned as the State over this inordinate passion for golf in St. Andrews and, by that time, in other parts of the country. Men were 'playing at the goff' when they should have been attending the church services. In 1598 the Kirk Session of St. Andrews Town Church admonished two of their congregation for this heinous act. It was complained that even the elders (church office-bearers) were neglectful of their duties because of it.

On the other hand, occasional archery did take place on the Links. In 1582, Patrick Learmont, son of a Provost of St. Andrews, took a pot shot at Archbishop Adamson who was disporting himself 'at the goff' when he should have been preaching!

Thus early the game had cast its spell over the land, ensnaring prince, prelate and peasant alike.

OBSESSION

Would you like to see a city given over
   Soul and body to a tyrannising game?
If you would there's little need to be a rover,
   For St. Andrews is the abject city's name.

It is surely quite superfluous to mention,
   To a person who has been here half-an-hour,
That golf is what engrosses the attention
   Of the people, with an all-absorbing power.

Rich and poor alike are smitten by the fever
   Their business and religion is to play;
And a man is scarcely deemed a true believer,
   Unless he goes at least a round a day.

The city boasts an old and learned college,
   Where you'd thnk the leading industry was Greek;
Even there the favoured instruments of knowledge
   Are the driver and a putter and a cleek.

All the natives and the residents are patrons
   of this royal, ancient, irritating sport;
All the old men, all the young men, maids and matrons—
   The universal populace in short.

R. F. MURRAY, 1885

THE Royal and Ancient game has a venerable and extensive bibliography, as to be expected from its antiquity. References in manuscripts, documents and paintings were indirect and incidental up to the 1600s. Almost unanimously since then the historical and literary records have emphasised one particular characteristic—the enslaving enchantment of the golf spell on its devotees at St. Andrews—obsession.

The city still lies happily subjugated and bewitched under that benign obsession. Its people have fought for almost a thousand years to retain their right of playing, and the passion has never relaxed its febrile grip. Now that the obsession is pandemic in the world, it does not appear so strange and unusual. When Murray, the old St.

Andrews student, wrote his verses a century ago, he was by no means the first to note this odd obsession of the St. Andrean, the native of St. Andrews. Nor was he the last.

The fever never abates and keeps on manifesting itself. It is perpetuated not merely in the myriad jokes, but in innumerable recorded incidents. In 1929 a big international golf final was being played on the Old Course. All St. Andrews seemed to be there watching a titanic struggle. The streets were deserted, apart from a solitary postman and a visitor. The latter was sight-seeing, with his camera at the ready, and obviously making for the ruined cathedral — in the opposite direction from the Links.

The postman neared the visitor, and, in passing, he muttered in words conjured up from the depths of gloom.

"She's five doon!" was all he said to the startled and mystified passer-by.

'She' was Joyce Wethered at the end of the first nine holes of the British Women's Amateur Championship against Glenna Collett. For the record, 'she', as described elsewhere, recovered to beat her American opponent by 3 and 2 to retain the championship for Britain. The postman was merely echoing the thoughts of all St. Andrews.

Another example of the total involvement of the population is given by Robert Harris, a distinguished former amateur champion and golf writer. He commented that the Old Course was the only arena in the world where white-capped maids and nurses were liable to topple out of the overlooking windows at an exciting championship finish. The day of white-capped maids is gone, but the interest remains.

Even in the simple and crude conditions for play before 1754 when the "Society" came to St. Andrews, golf was a fascinating and irresistible pastime. The 'Green', as the course was known for generations, then consisted of a ribbon-narrow strip of comparatively clear turf, surrounded by dense masses of whins. In the distance, without even a marking flag, was a clearer patch in the centre of which lay a roughly cut-out hole. After 'putting' down his ball the player teed up 'not less than a yard from the hole, not more than eight yards'. He drove off with his roughly contrived play club, using a pinnacle of sand to raise his ball, otherwise it could not have carried any distance over the surrounding hazards.

The earliest example of golf fever was Bishop Gavin Hamilton, an early Scottish prelate. He played a great deal on the Links of St. Andrews. One day "he became conscience-stricken when engaged in his usual golf. He went home, 'took bed instantlie and died, not having given any token of repentance for that wicked course he had embraced'".

Possibly the fact that he became conscience-stricken debars him from the ranks of the truly obsessed!

The above were the primitive conditions under which James Melville, son of a Montrose minister, according to his diary (1556-1601) played with "glubbes and bal" from the age of 7 years. He went to St. Andrews University in 1571 and records, "Though kept short of money, I had enough for archerie and goff. I had bow, arrose, glub and bals."

The Earl of March was Commendator of the Priory of St. Andrews. According to Melville, he "colluded with the revellers of the town to hold the ministrie of the Town Kirk vacant, and in the same tyme, tak up the stipend and spendit the same . . . at the goff, archerie, guid cheer, etc."

The great Duke of Montrose was the second historically recorded golf fanatic and had an early introduction to the game because his father had played before him. As a student at St. Andrews University in 1627, he was immediately in touch with "James Pett, the man who makes glubs". A number of references to his obsession for the game are contained in his student day expense accounts. A year later, having finished a match with the Laird of Luss, he becomes mindful of his matrimonial match with 'sweet Mistress Magdalene Carnegie'.

Next day he was married, on November 10, 1629; "but scarcely had the minstrels ceased to serenade them, when we find Montrose at his clubs and balls again." On the ninth day after his marriage there is a sum paid "To one going to St. Andrews for clubs and balls for my Lord".

Montrose was probably among the first golfers to play with the most improved ball up to that date — the "featherie". It was introduced about 1618. Before then, balls for the most part were crude affairs of leather and flock or of wood. Their life was brief.

The Old Course has known since then innumerable 'keen hands', 'fans', 'addicts', as they have been described from era to era. Many came to St. Andrews to live in order to devote all their leisure to the Links — even from other countries.

Probably the most golf-obsessed man to the exclusion of all else, in the leisured days of last century, was old Sutherland. A member of the R. and A., he practically lived between the Old Course and Musselburgh for years in the mid-century. "He made golf his life more thoroughly than any man we know", recorded Robert Chambers of him. Sutherland was not much of a player himself, but he approached immortality on two counts. The first was that he became the first steward (self-appointed) at a golf match in history. Secondly, when the bunker at the 15th, a few yards beyond the Cottage Bunker, was named after him, because "he spent more time in it than he did in his home."

Sutherland absolutely revered anyone with above-average golfing skill and time spent away from the course for him was time wasted. When Allan Robertson, 'the greatest of his day' died, Sutherland mourned after his funeral, "they may toll the bells and shut up the shops in St. Andrews for their greatest is gone."

His attention to promising young players was deeply paternal. One day, an opponent was about to drive off at the last hole; "to strike off" as they said then, when a boy appeared on the Swilcan Bridge in direct line.

"Stop, stop" shouted old Sutherland frantically, "Don't play upon him! He is a fine young golfer!"

It would have been a tragedy if a fine young golfer had been 'played upon', and maybe hit!

Introduced to a lady — a visitor from London, he greeted her, "How are you! Mr Glennie never played better than today. He was round in 106. A grand golfer!" The lady had never heard of golf nor of George Glennie, one of the finest golfers of the period and winner of many R. and A. trophies.

Next to playing himself, Sutherland loved watching the 'cracks'. Anything like levity from spectators he frowned on. One day an excursion train arrived from nearby Dundee and the people streamed out over the Links to the seaside. Sutherland strode forward, cleek in hand, and waved them frantically off the course. He turned to his friends watching the match: "It is disgraceful of the railway people bringing a parcel of uneducated brutes down here when they knew a real match was going on", he shouted, deadly serious. "Uneducated" merely meant they knew nothing of golf.

Of the same golden era of the early 19th century was Campbell, laird of Saddell. A great, all-round sportsman in his youth, and bonviveur throughout his life, he classed golf as the king of all pleasures. George Hughes, writing to his brother, author of "Tom Brown's Schooldays", referred to 'this golfmania' as he called the obsession. It could be a description of any 19th Hole throughout the world today.

"You have heard squires at their wine after a good run; bless you, they can't hold a candle to golfers. Most of the players were Scotch, and the earnestness with which they play is a caution. This is true. How in the evening each dilates on his own wonderful strokes, and the singular chances that befell him in the different parts of the 'green'—all under the pleasurable delusion that every listener is as interested in his game as he himself. How he tells of his long swipes, which he is not sure have ever been equalled, and of the perfect pitch with baffy or iron. And then the long putt—how beautifully the ball rolled over the smooth green up to the very lip of the hole, or more fortunate still, dropped into it. I remember Saddell saying, as he looked down at a fine putt that borrowed a little from the side of the undulating ground, and dribbled gently down, down, down, into the hole. 'What a splendid putt; in my time I have had the best grouse-shooting in Scotland, and the best salmon river, and the best deer-stalking, and I have kept the best hunters at Melton; but I am thankful to say I can now dream of a putt!'"

Another devotee such as Sutherland was Walkinshaw, his chief opponent and a left-hander. He also had an Old Course bunker named after him. This is the treacherous trap set into the hillside short of the 13th green. Walkinshaw spent all his days on the course, much of the day evidently in this bunker, because it was written of him that "he could neither stay out of it, nor keep out of it". The members began to refer to it as "Walkinshaw's Grave", and a century after his death it is still 'the Walkinshaw'.

The most noted 19th century member of the R. and A., and an enthusiastic golfer most of his 87 years was John Whyte Melville. He averaged three days a week of 36 holes per day for over seventy years and played two rounds in a gale of wind one day at the age of 83 years. First elected Captain of the R. and A. in 1823, he was uniquely honoured by being elected Captain again in 1883 — sixty years later, but died before taking office. For much of his life his caddie was Sandy Herd, grandfather of the 1902 Open Champion.

One of the best-known of golf-obsessed university professors was P. G. Tait, the father of Freddie Tait, a golfing hero of St. Andrews. 'The Professor' was a mathematician and philosopher of distinction at Edinburgh University. In St. Andrews, where he came to reside regularly each summer from 1868 for over thirty years, he was just 'the professor'. He was a scholar who found everything that he wanted of physical and mental recreation in golf. It was his favourite game long before his sons became first-class players.

'The Professor' thought nothing of playing five rounds in one day, his favourite one being the morning round at 6 o'clock. He wore out a few caddies in the course of the day. To him the great value of a caddie was that matches attended by caddies could play through those without. It helped him squeeze in more rounds! Not until young Freddie began to emerge as the finest amateur of his day, however, did Professor Tait begin on his innumerable experiments with balls and clubs on a scientific basis. He also wrote verse on golf.

Having played with the Morrises, father and son, and the Strath brothers, he often contended in later life that Young Tom Morris would have been an outstanding golfer in any era. This was when his own son was breaking course records all over the country!

Possessed of a highly developed sense of fun, it was in humorous mood that, having played all day, he organised a night match playing with phosphorescent balls. The party for this game included his wife,

Young Tom's Tombstone, Cathedral Cemetery *(Photo by G. M. Cowie)*

Freddie Tait drives off

(Photo by G. M. Cowie)

the great 19th-century scientist, Professor Huxley, and Professor Crum Brown. The result recorded was: "The idea is a success, and all went well until the 'Burn' was passed, when Professor Crum Brown found that his glove was aflame, and his hand was burned in getting it off. A chastened group returned."

Another attempt to play at night came in 1928 when members of the R. and A., on the eve of their Autumn meeting, enjoyed a frolic in a novel attempt at floodlit golf. Two holes were enough.

When advancing years prevented Tait from playing more than nine holes, his experiments on the flight of the ball increased. He observed that, without spin, a ball would not travel far or combat gravity to any extent; but the greater the spin the farther it travelled, to a remarkable extent. He also found that the centre of gravity of a ball seldom coincided with the ball's actual centre.

Most ironic of his theories was that a ball could only be hit to carry a certain distance—about 190 yards. In 1892, soon after he propounded it, his own son, Freddie, exploded the theory with his record drive of 341 yards at the 13th hole of the Old Course. His gutta carried 250 yards!

Of the incident, young Tait wrote to a friend:— "I was at the University for an hour today with the Guv'nor, driving golf balls for him. He thinks he has now settled the whole thing. 215 feet per second he makes out to be the initial velocity of a golf ball. At one time he had it nearly up to 400 feet per second!"

Later:— "The Guv'nor will be very much annoyed (at his record 341 yard drive) as he wrote not very long ago an article to "Golf" proving conclusively that it was impossible to carry more than 190 yards on a calm day, unless you exert three times more energy."

Professor Knight of St. Andrews University showed his obsession for golf in a different way but with an equally academic approach. When not actually playing, he devoted some of his leisure to the amusing occupation of proving that Shakespeare, according to his works, was by no means unaware of the game of golf, and used many golfing allusions as colourful descriptions in his plays.

Throughout the subsequent years, innumerable extreme examples of 'golfmania' have, of course, occurred all over the world. A recent

St. Andrews one was when an attractive young New Zealand girl casually visited the town, fell under the spell of its golf links, and stayed for two years, devoting her full time to playing golf and absorbing herself in golfing lore. As casually as she came, she went. One day she spent, as usual, with a morning round, and then practice in the afternoon. The next day, without warning of any kind, she had gone.

In 1951, on September 17th, there arrived at the Old Course, Ralph Kennedy, one of the most obsessed and single-minded golfers in America. He had played 2999 golf courses all over the world. His ambition was to reach 3000 and to make the Old Course of St. Andrews the vital 3000th. This he did with a round duly testified by starter Jimmy Alexander.

The utter subjugation of a whole community to a game could not fail to excite literary notice throughout the years.

Apart from Hughes, travelled scholars like Lord Cockburn, and Smollett had commented wonderingly on it. The Society of Golfers themselves, comprising some of the most distinguished men in Scotland, bore legal witness to it. They drafted a legal plea, about 1800, for one of the many lawsuits involving the Old Course. It contained the following: —

> "The Links of St. Andrews have, from time immemorial been used by the inhabitants and others for the exercise of golf. From very early times a Society known by the name of the Golfing Society of St. Andrews, consisting of the most respectable inhabitants and the gentlemen of the County, had regularly made fixed payments for the purpose of golfing on the Links. This institution has been extremely useful to the town and has always met with great encouragement from the magistrates. This may have contributed to render the exercise so fashionable as it is, though it seems pointed out by nature as the most proper exercise for the inhabitants of that city. The smooth downs stretching along the seashore give the strongest invitation to an amusement so conducive to health.
>
> *"But whatever causes may be assigned for the fact, nothing can be more certain than that the exercise of golf is preferred to all others at St. Andrews, and generally considered as a sort of necessary of life."*

R. F. Murray was only one of innumerable poets to write of the obsession; a passion that made a recent journalist describe St. Andrews as "The city of magnificent obsession!"

Smollett observed that 'of this diversion the Scots are so fond that, when the weather will permit, you may see a multitude of all ranks, mingled together in their shirts, and following the balls with the utmost eaagerness.'

In 1874 Lord Cockburn wrote that the 'natives' 'have a pleasure of their own which is as much the staple of the place as old colleges and churches are. This is golfing which is here not a mere pastime, but a business and a passion, and has for ages been so, owing probably to their admirable links. . . . There is a pretty large set who do nothing else, who begin in the morning and stop only for dinner; and who, after practising the game in the sea breeze, discuss it all night. Their talk is of holes'.

Times change but not golfers!

SOCIETY OF ST. ANDREWS GOLFERS

THE first association formed for the playing of golf in St. Andrews was, of course, the Royal and Ancient Club. It came into existence in 1754 as the Society of St. Andrews Golfers, and received the Royal Prerogative in 1834 when the name was duly changed to its present familiar form.

At this point another understandable misconception must be corrected. The Royal and Ancient Golf Club is not the St. Andrews Golf Club. An important institution of that name exists in the city as the oldest artisan or tradesmen's club in the world. It has a unique and illustrious history of its own to which full reference is made later.

The Royal and Ancient Golf Club, administrators of golf, and the St. Andrews Golf Club, are two distinct and separate entities. They possess their respective club premises facing each other at diagonally opposite corners of the Home Green of the Old Course. Their only connecting links are the Links of St. Andrews.

The original minute book of the R. and A. explains why the aristocratic Society of Golfers, first naturally centred on the capital city, Edinburgh, came to St. Andrews. We read: –

> "The noblemen and gentlemen above named (twenty-two in all and most of them landed proprietors from different parts of Fife) being Admirers of the Anticient (*sic*) and healthful Exercise of the Golf, and at the same time, having the Interest and prosperity of the Anticient City of St. Andrews at heart, being the Alma Mater of the Golf, did in 1754 Contribute for a silver club . . . having a St. Andrew engraved on the head thereof to be played for on the Links of St. Andrews upon the 14th Day of May of said year, and yearly in time coming. . . ."

By its handsome recognition of St. Andrews as the traditional Home of Golf, the Society of Golfers of St. Andrews conferred a considerable boon on the little city. It has continued to do so bountifully during its tenure of the St. Andrews Links. The Club has helped St. Andrews to prosperity and prestige by making it the world's headquarters of golf administration. The choice of the town by the Club was apt, and it has been happy. The town and Links, of course, have ideally suited the Club, although, as with all marriages, the two parties have had at times to bear and forbear with each other. They have done so with success.

From its earliest days the Society comprised men of influence and wealth from all over Scotland whose common bond was the love of golf. In the 18th and 19th centuries they made golf essentially a patrician game. Its exponents were enviously or contemptuously described as 'having mair sillar nor sense'. They first gathered together sporadically to play at St. Andrews because of the eminent suitability of its Links; at Leith because of its proximity as the nearest golfing ground to Edinburgh, and at convenient seaside links near their own estates. ('Sillar' is Scots for money.)

The cost of the feather ball in the early days was a restricting economic factor on play by the local people although golf had been played traditionally by them for centuries. Another was the exclusiveness of the societies of golfers, of which St. Andrews was only one. This tended to keep the *hoi polloi* off the Links. It was the era of the Corinthian and the patrician. They played their games, foursomes generally among themselves. Just as important to them were the wagers and bets that were made on their matches. Some of the bets were as weird and far-fetched as the high gambling spirit of the times encouraged. They wined and dined heavily afterwards, and many of the matches and wagers were arranged '*in vino*'.

As typical of the bets recorded, here are two from their betting book: In 1819 —

> "Sir David Moncrieffe backs his life against the life of John Whyte-Melville for a new Silver Club, as a present to the St. Andrews Golf Club (Society of Golfers) the price of the club to be paid by the survivor, and the arms of the parties to be engraved on the club, and the present bet inscribed on it." — The bet was paid 13 years later by Mr Whyte-Melville who handed over a silver putter, one of the three symbolic clubs still in ceremonial use.

1822: — "Mr Bruce bets he will produce a leg of mutton (blackface) against the September meeting of the Club, superior to one to be produced by Mr Haig of Seggie, for a magnum of port to the Club. — Taken by Mr Haig".

Also in the spirit of the times, a distinctive uniform was a *sine qua non*. These were colourful and flamboyant, with specially designed buttons, and expensive material. Uniforms continued spasmodically throughout the years. Much later, fashion swung right round for a time when they were 'out' and it was the done thing to play in a favourite old jacket and odd trousers. The uniforms have come back in more recent years as club 'blazers'.

The Golfing Societies found they needed rules of play for certain situations that often arose, in order to settle their wagers. Meeting places soon became essential as well, and the inns and adjacent drinking parlours were not comfortable or private enough. Then followed organised competitions, and handicaps, and later also golf clubhouses were born.

The St. Andrews Society of Golfers foregathered first at an old tavern, the Black Bull, and later at the Union Parlour as an informal clubhouse. The informality is reflected in the fact that although minutes were kept, no other office-bearers were elected in the early years than a captain. He was the winner of the annual competition for the Silver Club before the honour became elective fifty years later. Until 1835 they even had no clubhouse until the Union Parlour was inaugurated on the site of the red sandstone building that stands prominently in a position diagonally opposite the present clubhouse.

It was this Society of Golfers which became, without seeking, the ruling body of golf. The responsibility was thrust upon it.

SIGNIFICANT DEVELOPMENTS

THE initial action of the Society of St. Andrews Golfers following their formation was to draw up rules for play. Most of them were also members of the Honourable Company of Edinburgh Golfers and they decided to adopt the code of thirteen rules which that body had drafted ten years earlier as the first circulated rules for the playing of golf.

The thirteen rules of the first code were: —

ARTICLES AND LAWS IN PLAYING THE GOLF.

1. You must tee your ball within a club length of the hole.
2. Your tee must be upon the ground.
3. You are not to change the ball which you strike off the tea (*sic*).
4. You are not to remove stones, bones or any break club for the sake of playing your ball except upon the fair green and that only within a club-length of your ball.
5. If your ball come among water, or any watery filth, you are at liberty to take out your ball, and throwing it behind the hazard 6 yards at least, you may play it with any club, and allow your adversary a stroke for so getting out your ball.
6. If your balls be found anywhere touching one another, you are to lift the first ball, till you play the last.
7. At holeing, you are to play your ball honestly for the hole, and not to play upon your adversary's ball, not lying in your way to the hole.
8. If you should lose your ball by its being taken up, or any other way, you are to go back to the spot where you struck last, and drop another ball, and allow your adversary a stroke for the misfortune.
9. No man at holeing his ball, is to be allowed to mark his way to the hole with his club or anything else.

10. If a ball be stop't by any person, horse, dog or any thing else, the ball so stop't must be played where it lyes.

11. If you draw your club in order to strike, and proceed so far in the stroke as to be bringing down your club; if then your club shall break, in any way, it is to be accounted a stroke.

12. He whose ball lyes furthest from the hole is obliged to play first.

13. Neither Trench, Ditch or Dyke made for the preservation of the Links, Nor the Scholars' Holes or the Soldiers' Lines, shall be accounted a hazard, but the Ball is to be taken out, Teed and played with any iron club.

The rules appear to have been adopted *en bloc* by the St. Andrews Society, retaining the phrase 'the Scholars' Holes' and the Soldiers' Lines' in Rule 13. As J. B. Salmond points out, both hazards existed at Leith, but, while there were 'Scholars' Holes' at St. Andrews, there were certainly no 'Soldiers' Lines'.

A natural development would have been for the Honourable Company to emerge as the responsible body; to promulgate their rules and to administer in the case of any subsequent amendments and additions. But, as the St. Andrews Society prospered and expanded, there was a decline in the Honourable Company with a waning interest in golf around Edinburgh, most of their members appearing to prefer the highly suitable amenities of St. Andrews. This was the development that led to the St. Andrews Society's later leadership in the administration of the game.

Golf at the time, by any standards, was an incredibly elementary and crude game, played over a sterile wasteland of heather and whin interspersed by clear areas of short sea-grass. The Society's sole interest, when they first came to St. Andrews, was in playing social matches among themselves in a pastime they found agreeable and amusing. In doing so, the members adopted a somewhat esoteric method of arriving at the result of these games. The scoring was based entirely on the number of holes won, whether over a single round, or any agreed number of rounds of the course. The number of strokes taken for a hole was a minor concern, and these were only noted in order to determine the winner of the hole. Whether a four or a fourteen won the hole, did not matter.

This is not as incredible as it may seem to the modern player, when one takes into account the crude conditions and the innumerable hazards that encircled the narrow path of the Old Course from tee to hole. These included possible rabbit scrapes on the green itself, and dense foliage on either side of the ribbon-narrow fairway, or fair-green. The putting, or play-green, itself was only roughly prepared. The rough-and-ready hole often became so deep that it was difficult to rescue balls from it. While singles were occasionally played, the Society favoured foursome matches in which the members of each side played alternate strokes. This, the Scottish Foursome, continued until the First World War as the favourite game for four players with most golf clubs, until ousted by the increasing urge for individual competitive play, and the four-ball game.

The number of holes comprising the few golf courses in the country at the time varied from locality to locality. Until 1764 the Old Course possessed twelve, and a round comprised 22 holes. Players started by driving off within about two club-lengths of the last hole (note hole, not green), played eleven out, and then went back on their tracks, playing back on the same holes.

That year the Society decided to compress the first four holes into two, so making a round of 18 holes. The choice of 18 was quite fortuitous and was dictated entirely by the layout available, but the other existing golf links in Scotland gradually followed suit; subsequent courses that were laid out were also designed for 18 holes thus that number became the accepted standard round.

In his reminiscences about 1860 Robert Chambers wrote: —

"Golf, like all other games, has its especial phraseology. Thus, he who is about to play the same number of strokes as his antagonist has already played, plays 'the like'; if he is about to play one stroke more than his rival has already played, he plays 'the odd'; if one stroke less, he plays 'one off two'; if two strokes more, 'two more' and so on. This method of reckoning, though somewhat confusing at first, is, after a little time, easily acquired; and, for its being universally adopted on golf courses, should receive especial attention . . . the round is gained by the player who has achieved the greater number of holes. It is not unfrequent for each player to have gained an equal number of holes during the round; nor is it of very unfrequent occurrence to see round after round halved, the contesting parties leaving off even at the end of the day's play. . . . A match may consist of a certain number of holes, independently of rounds, when it, of course, accrues to the winner of the greater number of holes. In important matches the latter is the usual method for deciding the relative skill of rival players; and in contests between professional players the match usually consists of a certain number of holes to be contested on more links than one.

"The number of strokes taken between each hole depends on the skill of the player, the distance to be traversed, and the nature – hazardous or otherwise, of the intervening ground. . . . If it is agreed that the match shall fall to the player who holes the entire round in the fewest strokes, as in playing for Medals, each stroke is scrupulously recorded; but if the match is to be yielded to the winner of the greatest number of holes in a round, the number of strokes need not necessarily be recorded.

". . . Those links which possess no hazards are considered inferior to those on which they plentifully occur, and it may be stated that on difficult links it requires more real golfing science to avoid driving balls into, than out of, hazards. Hazards consist of sand-pits (bunkers), gorse or whin bushes, cart-roads, long grass, water, etc.; as a ball must, with certain exceptions, be played where it lies, the avoidance of hazards constitutes much of the superiority of an excellent player."

The earliest known survey of the Old Course was made in 1821. It shows the area of the Links that was purchased from the Town Council of St Andrews at that time, by James Cheape of adjoining Strathtyrum, with the Old Course maked off with boundary stones to distinguish it from the remainder of the Links. The plan is produced in this volume as an end-paper, and gives the names of the ten holes then in use (nine out and then back).

Hole o' Hill was sited just west of the Sandie Track (Grannie Clark's Wynd). Players drove off from beside it, and the hole itself came into use as the last hole of the round.

From there, the golfer drove down to Bridge Hole, across the Swilcan Burn, the distance being given as 261 yards; the second was 'Cunnin Hole' (Rabbit Hole) (436 yards); then followed 'Cartgate' (328 yards). The fourth was 'Ballfield Hole' (387 yards); fifth 'Hole o' Cross' (303 yards); sixth 'Muir Hole' (370 yards); 7th 'Eden Hole' (330 yards); 8th 'Hole o' Turn' (132 yards); and 9th 'End Hole' (302 yards). The total distance of the course was given as three miles, four furlongs, 218 yards. The width varied from 72 yards to 193 yards, the average being 140 yards.

The 4th Hole, in Chambers' day, which was some thirty-odd years after this survey of 1821, was better known as 'The Ginger Beer' because it was there that a stall was erected and ginger beer (generally laced with brandy from the clubhouse) was sold; the 5th was invariably known as 'Hell' because of its huge bunker of that name, of which P. P. Alexander at the time parodied in a verse, "Abandon hope all ye who enter here." The 6th was The Heather Hole, because of its expanse of bare heather fairway, with a green that was as much sand as grass. Not for many years after was a proper turf green laid there. The 'Eden' was the High Hole, where 'The shelly pit is cleared at one fell blow'. The 8th was by now generally just referred to as 'The Short' rather than the 'Hole o' Turn'. 'The End' had no other name.

Until its abolition in 1951 the stymie had remained a highly controversial ruling from the first recordings of golf as a game. Originally, when opposing balls finished up anywhere on the course near each other a 'stimie' had occurred. The word is derived from the old Scots word 'stime', meaning a hindrance of vision. The custom prior to rules becoming established in 1744, was that an adversary could 'play his opponent's ball' in the case of being stymied, whether on the 'hole green' or the 'fair green'. This meant that he could hit it indirectly in playing his own, as hard as he liked. The opportunities for gamesmanship were, of course, obvious. They resulted in many a fierce argument, and worse!

Therefore, it became a ruling of prime importance in shaping the development of golf when the St. Andrews Society of Golfers decreed in 1787 that there was only a 'stimie' position when the balls were six inches or more apart, otherwise the impeding ball must be lifted.

This lifting was important, because it was a departure from the basic principle of the ancient game that a ball must be played where it lay. Accordingly, the opportunity to attack an opponent's ball was virtually abolished, while the right to obstruct it was still retained – the stymie.

Even that right was regularly attacked as being unfair. Chambers commented that "it is not considered quite fair to play intentionally so as to lay a stimie; but in practice they very frequently occur, and often cause a hole to be halved which the stymied man felt confident of winning."

In 1883 Sir H. L. Playfair, member of the Society and the noted Provost of St. Andrews, had a motion carried to the effect that in future the 'stimie' should be abolished and that all balls on the putting green (a rough area around 20 yards of the hole) should be lifted at the option of the player. Some fifty years later a Professor in the University wrote:

> "The fine old 'stimie' can well be spared along with the fine old prize fight, and the fine old cottage, innocent of ventilation and balmy with fine old odours. It must not be granted the privilege of fine old port, fine old ladies, and fine old customs and institutions, which have some poetry, meaning and nobility of purpose about them. The 'stimie' is distinctly ignoble."

Commenting on the rule some 70 years ago, H. S. C. Everard, the noted R. and A. historian, suggested prophetically: – "Perchance, in another hundred years or so, the six-inch limit may be further extended or, who knows, the stimie disestablished altogether!"

The stymie was introduced again at the end of the experimental twelve months of 1833, but it remained under persistent attack throughout the years until the Professor's words became the general opinion and the stymie was abolished in 1951, this time forever.

The retention of the stymie for so long struck many as a clear case of a reactionary regard for tradition for its own sake that was not in the interests of the game's development.

Apart from this highly controversial issue on rules, the keen players in the Golfing Society began to see the greater justice of counting by strokes rather than holes won, and in 1759 they agreed to adopt the method of stroke or medal play to decide the winner of their Silver Club with which went the honour of captaincy. Among other things, this established for the records the finest round of golf played for almost a century. It was a score of 94 made by James Durham of Largo which won the 1767 R. and A. Silver Putter. Durham's portrait, believed to be by Raeburn, hung in the St Andrews Council Chamber for many years until it was loaned to the Royal and Ancient Club for hanging there.

Durham's round remained a record for 86 years, into the days of the much superior gutta ball. It was an amazing achievement on the constricted, rough-and-ready Old Course of the day, with its untended greens, unprepared tees, and path-like fairways. Comparable with it in the 19th century was when Allan Robertson, the acknowledged master golfer of his time, became the first man to break eighty (with the gutta ball, of course) in 1858. A modern comparison would be breaking the existing course record of 65 by two or three clear shots!

Captaincy of the Society of Golfers was made elective in 1806, instead of the honour going to the winner of the Silver Club. It was then there began the tradition of the captain-elect playing a ceremonial drive from the first tee to ensure possession of the Silver Club and the captaincy. By this time, greenkeepers had been appointed to make conditions easier for the golfers by improving the Old Course. It was widened in 1832 in order to convert the small greens into huge, double greens so that players could aim at holes cut in the west part of the greens going out, and the east side on returning.

These double greens are still the unique and outstanding feature of the Old Course today. Their sole purpose was to relieve the congestion caused by a steadily increasing number of golfers, by the economical creation of 18 separate holes and fairways.

"A round is requiring as much as three to four hours with much tedious waiting" was a recorded complaint. A speedy game was golf then, two hours being average for the nine-out-and-back circuit.

A threat to the Links in 1845 was the coming of the railway, which it was proposed should cut through the Old Course at the Burn Hole. The Club were successful in having the line diverted to avoid this, and in 1851 the railway line skirted the course for a matter of 300 yards. The rails were lifted in 1968 and the deserted track is still a hazard; the protective fencing still marks the boundaries of the Old and Eden courses.

34

"ROYAL AND ANCIENT"

THE Society of Golfers of St. Andrews became the Royal and Ancient Golf Club in 1834, by grant of King William IV. Three years later the King further bestowed his favour by presenting a Gold Medal to be played for annually. It has continued to be the chief award at the Club's Autumn meetings.

In the following year the widowed Queen Adelaide presented a gold medal bearing her name, with a request that it should be worn by the Captain of the Club on all public occasions. The original trophy, the Silver Club, was supplemented, of necessity, by a second one in 1819, as it had become overloaded with the silver balls annexed traditionally to it by successive captains. It was donated in a bet by John Whyte-Melville who golfed for over 70 years until he was in his eighties. This gifting process had to be repeated in 1922 when the late Duke of Windsor, captain of that year as Prince of Wales, presented a replica of the original trophy to the Club.

Some years after 1834 came the first-ever step towards the organisation of competitive golf on an established basis.

On the initiative of the Prestwick Club members, the R. and A. consented to combine with them and the Honourable Company of Edinburgh in 1860 to provide a trophy in the organising of an open golf championship to decide 'the best golfer in the world'. The trophy, a handsome and ornate belt, became the outright property of Young Tommy Morris of St. Andrews under the conditions of the championship when he won it for the third time in a row in 1870. The event lapsed until a new trophy was provided two years later. The first winner was again the son of Tom Morris, making his fourth successive win of the championship. He died three years later at the age of 24 years.

The spell of golf was now taking a wider hold throughout Britain. By 1875 Robert Clark, Edinburgh, himself a member of the R. and

A. and author of a significant early historical work on golf, was able
to record: —

> "The admitted supremacy of St. Andrews as a golfing centre
> may in various ways be accounted for. Socially and otherwise
> the place has always been a pleasant one. Even in its decay some
> savour of the ancient prestige continues to cling to it. For the
> purposes of the game of golf the Links are, on the whole,
> unrivalled by any other Links in Scotland. . . . The Royal and
> Ancient may now be fairly called, without dispute, the 'National
> Club of Scotland'. Nearly all golfers of note are members!'"

Clark took no account of the artisan spread of golf, even although
professionalism had begun to make a strong impact on the game. His
reference was only to 'gentleman' golfers. Soon the Royal and
Ancient was to become the recognised authority and arbiter on all
questions of golf wherever the pastime was played. Increasingly golf
was being referred to as 'the Royal and Ancient game'.

In 1885 the Royal Wimbledon Club approached the R. and A.
with the request that it should take steps to form an association of
golf clubs. These were springing up all over Britain and overseas as
the game's popularity continued to mount at a phenomenal rate. The
chief purpose of the association was that its members should play
under one uniform code of rules.

Accordingly the R. and A. formed a special committee of its own
members, along with delegates from other clubs, to carry this out. In
1888 they issued a set of rules to all known clubs and left it at that.
But four years later came a further and stronger agitation for one
single authority. The Association of Golf Clubs proposed that the R.
and A. alone should legislate. The Club then, with unanimous
approval, appointed 15 of its own members as a Rules of Golf
Committee.

Thus it was that the Royal and Ancient Club finally became, in
name, as it had already long been in fact, the ruling body in golf,
accepted by clubs and players all over the world. Unification of the
American and British codes of rules at St. Andrews in 1951 was the
final great step forward towards international unity. The R. and A.
and the United States Golf Association maintain constant
consultations on fundamental issues.

Clearly, the town of St. Andrews owes much to the Society of Golfers for its present-day prestige, but the Club is even more indebted to St. Andrews because of the city's recognition as the traditional Home of Golf. There the wisdom of golfing experience of centuries had accumulated and been handed down from one generation to another long before 1754.

But the very popularity of the game was bringing in its train domestic problems and worries due, by 1890, to the spate of new golfers arriving on the St. Andrews scene. Visitors were pouring in increasingly with each successive year.

It has to be realised that the privilege of playing golf in St. Andrews was truly unique in that it was free to all . . . resident, R. and A. member, and casual visitor alike. This was no calculated scheme to popularise golf. It was the maintenance of an ancient right.

Once again congestion was becoming intolerable on the Old Course. Members of the R. and A. which paid for the maintenance the Course under the old agreement with the town's administrators were actually being crowded out on occasion! The Club came to a major decision that the time had come to possess their own course in St. Andrews. The members negotiated in 1893 to buy the ancient Links, including the Old Course from Mr Cheape, the laird of the adjoining estate of Strathtyrum, into whose possession they had come.

The townspeople re-acted violently against the proposed purchase by the R. and A. They expressed outrage and a determination to buy back for themselves their ancient birthright which had been sold some hundred years earlier.

Commenting on this situation in his books on "The Links", Dr Hay Fleming, the noted local historian wrote: —

"Few small cities have so many attractions to offer to a resident population or to summer visitors as St. Andrews; but the Links easily outweigh all the other attractions combined — education, sea-bathing, interesting ruins and historical associations. To the material prosperity of the City the Links are very vital indeed. The questions at issue affect, directly or indirectly, every St. Andrews proprietor and householder, whether they are golfers or not. The present course is already far too restricted for the demands made upon it in the summer. With the well-deserved and rapidly increasing popularity of the game, it may be safely stated that two or even three courses would be none too many for the Metropolis of golf. . . . In the past the Town and the Club have got on well together, and he would be no true friend to either who would try to set them by the ears. The Club have done much for the Course in recent years, but . . . the Club have not done everything. . . . Should the Club acquire the superiority of the Links, and form a new course, it could not be expected that that course should be thrown open to all and sundry. So long as it was in a rough and rugged state, outsiders indeed would be welcomed, that their play might help to bring it into condition; but once the new course was in good order, it may be safely assumed that non-members would be debarred, if possible. That would not be the only evil. With a good private course of their own, the Club would stop their lavish expenditure on the present course. The other local players could not possibly keep it up for the multitudes who choose to take the use of it; and if not upheld it would soon become unplayable. As a matter of absolute necessity the Town Council would require to step in then and it is surely much better that they should do so now."

These were the town's views, and the Club finally withdrew from the sale after protracted negotiations. Out of these was born a new arrangement between the parties, guaranteeing the Club certain privileges and demanding certain duties of course maintenance by the Club. This was enacted in a Parliamentary Order which has subsequently been amended from time to time to suit changing circumstances in the same way as the new Links Trust has been born. Out of the situation also, arose the formation of another course on the Links, appropriately named the New Course. Contiguous to the Old, it was opened in 1895 and was very soon a first-class golf course.

Despite this controversy and its protracted and heated legal proceedings, relations between the Club and the Town have always remained good, with the R. and A. carrying out the sentiment expressed in their original minute of 'having the interest and prosperity of the ancient city of St. Andrews at heart'. As an instance, in 1899 they instituted a competition and presented a gold medal for the local players' championship of the Links. The only stipulation was that competitors must be members of a town club. The St. Andrews, Thistle and Guild Clubs then were the only three with a complete organisation and the recognised standing. The New Club was subsequently added. The first winner of the R. and A. Medal in 1890 was Sandy Herd, later to become an Open Champion. Lawrence and Joseph Auchterlonie won it in the next two years respectively, both future international ambassadors of the game.

Not until 1919 did the Royal and Ancient Club take over the complete management of the Open and the Amateur Championships, the organisation of which, more and more, had been left to them. Under the wise guidance of their Championship Committee several innovations compelled by modern conditions included the first levying of a charge on spectators, and later on, as the galleries of spectators swelled, various methods of crowd control. The innovations brought the running of these and other events now under their charge to its present high level. St. Andrews was the first place where crowd control by roping off the spectators from the players was tried, in 1939.

In the subsequent years to 1919 the Club had, as captains, no fewer than three royal brothers, the sons of King George V. They were the Prince of Wales (Duke of Windsor), 1922; Duke of York (King George VI), 1930, and the Duke of Kent, 1937.

The Walker Cup contests with America in Britain were also in their control, and there is local satisfaction that the two British successes in the series so far have been gained on the Old Course in 1938 and 1971.

At the conclusion of the war, General Eisenhower, C.-in-C. Allied Forces was elected an honorary member of the R. and A. and played a hurried round of the Old Course. Five years later a gracious and diplomatic gesture was the election as Captain of Francis Ouimet, the first American to be so honoured. His portrait was presented to the Club by Bobby Jones, one of its distinguished golfing members, and it now hangs there. Mr Joseph C. Dey, Chief Executive of the USGA, was elected Captain in 1975.

The bicentenary of the Club in 1954 was celebrated fittingly with a dinner in St. Andrews Town Hall, the right of the Club to use of the hall being a traditional one it rarely exercises.

A slightly uneasy alliance with the Town in the management of the Links arising out of the 1894 agreement was much improved in 1953 when a Joint Links Committee of Town and R. and A. representatives took over the control of the courses with considerable success and efficiency. But in 1970 Lord Wheatley produced his Report on the Reform of Local Government in Scotland. It was a far-reaching Report which recommended that Town and County Councils should be abolished and replaced by a two-tier system of local government by Regional and District Councils. Of vital concern to Fife was his proposal that the northern part of the County should be administered by Tayside, and the southern part by the Lothians. It seemed that control of the municipally owned golf courses would pass from St. Andrews to some remote authority in Dundee or Edinburgh.

Local Golf Clubs, notably the New Club and the Royal and Ancient, told St. Andrews Town Council that they would align themselves with any consortium which the Town Council might institute to keep control of the courses in local hands. Consultations followed, and as a result the 1974 Links Order Confirmation Act went through Parliament. The effect of this was the setting up of a St. Andrews Links Trust to hold the Links and formulate policy; and a Links Management Committee to deal with the day-to-day running of the courses. The golf Links belong to North East Fife District Council with Headquarters in Cupar. Fife County Council had successfully opposed the proposal to split the County, and the Plan of Reorganisation was altered to keep Fife as a Region in its own right.

One of the first actions of the Links Trust was to restore the office of Caddie Master, for it was becoming more and more necessary to restrict the use of caddie-carts on the courses, particularly the Old. Mr J. W. Winskell, a former RAF Warrant Officer, took command of the new emerging breed of golf caddie.

But the Links Trust had other problems. St. Andrews Town Council had failed to solve the problem of changing accommodation for visiting golfers. For many years golfers had used the converted

Bay Tea Room overlooking the Bruce Embankment, but it was less than adequate. In some respects it was a forbidding building. The iron gates which clanged behind the visitor had rather more than a hint of "Sing-Sing". Planning restrictions and financial stringencies had combined to thwart the efforts of the Town Council to find premises worthy of the Home of Golf.

In 1981 the Links Trust purchased Rusack's Marine Hotel, a four-star hotel which looks across the 1st and 18th fairways of the Old Course. They had, rather reluctantly, become hoteliers. The main object of the purchase was to convert the lower ground floor of the hotel into a Links Rooms complex. With financual aid from the Scottish Tourist Board the complex was opened in 1983. It provides a lounge where meals and drinks can be served; a "Spike" room where drinks can also be dispensed; changing rooms with toilets, showers and locker rooms; and a functions room where golfers visiting in a party may have their own privacy.

R. AND A. TRADITIONS

FOUNDED in the days when ceremony was important and elaborate, and when special uniforms for playing golf were part of this ceremony, the Royal and Ancient Club has acquired a number of traditions in the course of more than 200 years' existence. At the annual dinners during the Autumn meeting, the three silver putters, festooned heavily with the silver balls of the Captains (gold in the case of Royal Captains), are displayed in front of the head table where sit the former captains in their red coats.

Once the captain-elect has been duly installed, new members file past and kiss the symbolic clubs. These, draped in the blue and white of the Club's colours, are carried before the Captain on national occasions and when the members have occasion to take part in processions through the streets of the town. They are draped solemnly in black for funerals, but the member so honoured must be buried within the city boundaries of St. Andrews, for the clubs and balls must not be taken beyond those limits.

Dr Thomas Frognall Dibdin, in 1836, describes graphically a visit to St. Andrews when he attended the annual dinner and ball held by the Society of Golfers during their Autumn meeting. The Captain of the Club, Major Belshes, presided, and along with other members, wore a short red coat with dark blue collar — the uniform of the Captain and past-Captains.

> Dibdin goes on: "After dinner the mysteries were entered upon. The silver baton, staff or club (there was only one in those days) which is used to propel the ball onwards, was placed on the table before the President; having silver balls . . . fastened to the body of the baton. Then came a shorter silver club, called a putter, also encircled by silver balls. The candidate, on his admission to the Golfing Club by ballot, comes forward to the side of the President who, raising the putter aloft, the former courteously receives it, and kisses one or more of the balls."

Describing the match on the following day, the day of the Medal, Dibdin says:

> "The game of golf is played on what are called The Links, or upon an uneven greensward near the sea. The Links of St. Andrews are considered to be the finest in Scotland. . . . The game of which I was a personal witness . . . is carried on with great keenness; and is composed of the 'outward' and the 'inward' course; that is to say, of the number of strokes given in holing the ball outwards, and doing the same inwards; in the whole 18 holes. It is played in partnership or alone. Each champion is vigilantly attended by a marker, and to obtain the game within 90 strokes is considered to be the performance of a master in the art or craft of Golfing. The game I saw was not got under 104 strokes; 55 out and 49 in. Major Wemyss was the champion. At starting a little boy raises a very small portion of dirt — perhaps three inches in height, upon the top of which the ball is placed, and from whence the first stroke is made, which is generally a very long one."

Another tradition of the Club, more spectacular, but not quite so old, is the formal driving-in of the Captain each Autumn. This dates from the year 1806, when the Captaincy was made elective. At eight o'clock of a September morning (formerly October), the Captain-elect appears from the Clubhouse. He is supported by a retinue of former captains, and attended by the honorary professional. No matter how composed he may appear, and no matter how experienced a golfer, the Captain-elect is tense and anxious. Before him lies the greatest honour, but also one of the biggest ordeals in golf — that of making the ceremonial drive from the first tee of the world's oldest golf course, faced by a gallery comprising some of the world's most knowledgeable and competent players.

Down the fairway and across Grannie Clark's Wynd, the road which crosses the first and last fairways to the beach, are spread out the waiting caddies. The honorary professional tees up the Captain-elect's ball. Then, the cynosure of all eyes, he prepares to address himself to the drive that will automatically make him Captain. At the same moment, a tiny cannon booms out, startling even those steeled for its roar.

The lucky caddie who retrieves the ball from the scramble and free-for-all that ensues, runs to take it back to the Captain and from his hands receives as reward a golden sovereign. The wily caddies have long previously sized up the golfing abilities of the Captain-elect in positioning themselves to win the honour—and the sovereign. When the Duke of Windsor in 1922, played himself in as Captain of the Club, the late Sir Guy Campbell, a noted golf writer and golfer himself, recorded that some of the caddies "stood disloyally near the tee".

Sovereigns are now seldom minted, but the Royal and Ancient Club have been able to secure a dispensation enabling them to have a small supply of the now-rare coins struck in order to allow them to continue the traditional ceremony.

At the conclusion of the Spring and Autumn meetings of the Club, and of the golfing season for the members, comes another pleasing little ceremony. The tiny old-fashioned piece of artillery has been brought out of retirement for the occasion and stands near the starter's box and the first tee. It is ceremoniously fired, a miniature of sound and fury, as it was when the Captain played himself into office. The same procedure similarly marks the start and ending of the Spring meeting. In early days the Club borrowed a cannon from the town for the purpose (a cannon used by the townspeople in the long-since defunct ceremony of riding the marches). In 1859 the R. and A. acquired their own artillery.

How they did so mirrors another facet of the history of St. Andrews itself. Prior to the days of steam the notorious bar of the River Tay and the rock-bound coastline of St. Andrews Bay brought disaster to many sailing vessels. In April, 1858, the 1200 ton sailing ship, Sutlej, of Dundee, carrying a crew of 35 was driven on the rocks and foundered. It became a total wreck and by the time that the coast-guards arrived had been well plundered by the people of the Fife coast. The stores and gear remaining were sold later in St. Andrews by public auction, including the ship's armoury consisting of this little cannon. It was presented to Provost Playfair as a gift to St. Andrews. Through the good offices of the Provost, the town's greatest servant and benefactor of that century, it was acquired by the Club.

A joint tradition which the Royal and Ancient Club and the City of St. Andrews share is the annual match played each September between representatives of the two—affluents v. artisans. The R. and

A. members are highly hospitable hosts. At the conclusion of keenly fought games in which Lord So-and-so may find himself and his noble partner being soundly thrashed by the local gravedigger and plumber—or vice-versa—the town's team, comprising members of the local clubs, are liberally wined and dined at the 19th hole in the Clubhouse.

It may seem strange at first sight that the R. and A. have never had a full-time professional, but the bulk of the members play most of their golf at courses near their homes. For instance, many Americans are members, including, in 1966, 54 from the Pine Valley Club alone. In that year they presented to the Club the Pine Valley Trophy for play in the Autumn meeting. The position of professional therefore is a sinecure, and only one to act in an honorary capacity is needed. Since Tom Morris was appointed greenkeeper and professional in 1864 (the duties being almost solely those of greenkeeper) the Club has had a short but distinguished succession of professionals. Morris was the first to be appointed to the honorary post when he retired from active duties in 1904 at the age of 83 years. On his death he was succeeded by Andrew Kirkaldy also as honorary professional. After him came Willie Auchterlonie, another St. Andrews born Open Champion and he was succeeded on his death in 1964 in his 91st year by his son, Laurie, the well-known expert on clubmaking.

It is the duty of the honorary professional to tee the ball for the Captain-elect when he drives himself into office, and to await his return at the Home Green. Combined with these courtesy duties, he also gives the signal for the ceremonial firing of the cannon at the Club's bi-annual meetings.

A fact little-known, even in St. Andrews itself, concerns the nautical-looking flagstaff of the R. and A., located just behind the 18th green. It is an actual mast from that most famous of wind-jammers—the Cutty Sark.

A tradition that has remained inviolate against repeated assault is the rule that no women are admitted into the precincts of the Royal and Ancient Club. This goes back, of course, to the days when the thought that ladies ever would or could play golf was undreamed-of. "Men only" still remains the strict law of the Club. This rule is relaxed on special occasions to allow important visiting ladies to be officially received by the members and on other occasions such as St. Andrew's Day when the public is admitted to certain of the Club's offices. But the rule barring ladies from entering the Club as individual guests tolerates no exception.

GLORY REGAINED

St. Andrews, they say that thy glories are gone,
That thy streets are deserted, thy castles overthrown.
If thy glories be gone, they are only, methinks,
As it were, by enchantment, transferred to thy Links.
Though thy streets be not now, as of yore, full of prelates,
Of abbots and monks, and of hot-headed zealots,
Let none judge us rashly, or blame us as scoffers,
When we say that instead there are Links full of goffers.
With more of good heart and good feeling among them
Than the abbots, the monks, and the zealots who sung them.
We have red coats and bonnets, we've putters and clubs;
The green has its bunkers, its hazards and rubs.
At the long hole across we have biscuits and beer,
And the Hebes who sell it give zest to the cheer.
If this makes not up for the pomp and the splendour
Of mitres, and murders, and mass—we'll surrender.
If golfers and caddies be not better neighbours
Than abbots and soldiers, with crosses and sabres,
Let such fancies remain with the fool who so thinks,
While we toast old St. Andrews, its golfers and links.

George Fullarton Carnegie of Pitarrow (1813).

BEYOND question the most important factor in the phenomenal development of golf has been the improvement of successive balls.

The basic urge in all players . . . the urge that is the fatal fascination of the game . . . is 'hitting the ball out of sight'. In the earliest days balls were made of almost anything that could be turned or compressed into a spherical shape. Before 1618 they were made from roughly turned wood, or from flock, tightly bound in leather.

When the feather ball made its appearance about that year it was a tremendous advance on its primitive predecessors. By 1800 it was standardised as follows: "Balls are about 1¼ inches in diameter, and weigh from 26 to 30 drams. They are made of strong alumed leather, and stuffed with feathers. (A top hat full of feathers was the general measure.) The feathers are forced in at a small hole left in the covering, by a blunt-pointed instrument of iron which the maker applies to his shoulder, and the operation is continued until the balls acquire a degree of hardness and elasticity scarcely credible to those who have not seen it. When sufficiently dry, the balls are painted with white oil to exclude water and render them easily seen."

The family of Robertson, from which Allan, the first professional in the game, was descended, were traditional manufacturers of golf balls in St. Andrews for generations. Allan himself made balls that rivalled the famous 'Gourlays' from Musselburgh, the best ball of its time. In 1840, he turned out, assisted by Tom Morris, 1021 'featheries'; in 1841 a total of 1392, and in 1844, no fewer than 2456 balls. The making of 'featheries' was an arduous and wearisome business. It was also extremely unhealthy, and many ball-makers contracted lung trouble and asthma, that led to early deaths. This was the fate of many promising young artisan golfers.

While still new, a 'featherie' could be hit a very long way indeed. The record drive was achieved by a Frenchman, Samuel Messieux, who was a teacher of French at Madras College, St. Andrews, and became a fine golfer in the process, although it is recorded against him, a 'nervy' putter. In 1836 he drove 361 yards over the Elysian Fields, a stretch of the 14th hole . . . a tremendous hit even under the most favourable conditions. At their best and newest, the 'featheries' flew further than the 'guttas', but they soon lost their flight and their shape, as well as being much costlier. With its many qualities, chiefly those of price and durability, the gutta soon ousted its rival.

Chance, in the unlikely form of the Hindu god, Vishnu, produced the gutta, and with it the most revolutionary change in the whole history of golf. At the same time, it helped to snatch St. Andrews from the jaws of oblivion, and lead it back to prosperity and fame.

The elation of the artisan golfers of the time at the arrival of the gutta ball is clearly expressed in the following lines read at the Innerleven Club dinner in September, 1848.

IN PRAISE OF GUTTA PERCHA

Though gowff be of our games most rare,
Yet, truth to speak, the wear and tear,
o' balls was felt to be severe,
And source o' great vexation;
When *Gourlay balls cost half-a-croon,
And *Allan's no' a farthin' doun,
The feck o's wad been harried soon
In this era of taxation.

Right fain we were to be content
Wi' used-up balls new lickt wi' paint,
That ill-concealed baith scar and rent —
Balls scarcely fit for younkers (children).
And though our best wi' them we tried,
And nicely every club applied,
They whirred and fuffed, and dooked and shied,
And sklenkit into bunkers.

But times are changed, we dinna care,
Though we may ne'er drive leather mair,
Be't stuffed wi' feathers or wi' hair —
For noo we're independent.
At last a substance we hae got,
Frae which for scarce mair than a groat (4d)
A ba' comes that can roll and stot (bounce)
A ba' the maist transcendent.

* Gourlay of Musselburgh; Allan Robertson, St. Andrews

In the 1840s the glory of St. Andrews was indeed gone. The town was in debt to the tune of £10,000 . . . a vast sum then for a small community that was dwindling every year. The University had sunk to a handful of students; there had even been talk of moving it to Perth. By 1848 the links, the townspeople's heritage, had been illegally sold to the neighbouring landowner, Mr George Cheape, of Strathtyrum. Cholera, the black plague, had hit the town.

The fortunes of St. Andrews were at their lowest ebb.

But in that same year of 1848 the golf ball makers were persuaded only with greatest reluctance, to try out a new-fangled ball. The first examples were made from the gutta percha that enswathed a large black marble idol of Vishnu. It arrived in 1843 from Singapore, consigned to Dr Paterson of St. Andrews University. For months the strips of unfamiliar vegetable lay in his home where Robert Paterson, a younger son, was an impecunious student for the ministry. True St. Andrean, he was also an ardent golfer. But even second- and third-hand 'featheries' came hard on his pocket. The thrifty Scots family of Dr Paterson had found a use for the gutta percha. They utilised it to sole and heel their footwear!

Robert conceived still another use for it, and the first gutta ball started as a boot sole that was falling apart! He fashioned it into a rough sphere and fearfully used it in the early hours of an April morning in 1845 on the Old Course. His white-painted ball lasted only a few strokes. In painting it, he was far ahead of his time. For some years after their successful introduction, 'guttas' were used in their natural brown colour.

Young Paterson persevered. He passed the idea on to a brother at Lauder, near Edinburgh, who improved on it. He sent out a first batch of gutta balls, stamped 'Paterson's Composite Golf Ball', in 1846. They were exhibited also in London, but no one would look at them. In St. Andrews, Allan Robertson, of professionals, *facile princeps*, turned them down, afraid they would ruin his 'featherie' trade. But his assistant, Tom Morris, had second thoughts. This led to a split between the two best golfers of their day, and Morris decided to open his own shop, convinced of a rosy future for the cheaper and more durable gutta, and so for golf.

Even he never visualised how immensely the new ball would open up the game, bring fresh vitality and hope to his native town; would bring also a unique honour and fame to himself over a long life that spanned the rise of St. Andrews from poverty to a new peak of prosperity.

The smoothly moulded ball, it was soon found, flew better after being hacked and cut by use. An ingenious saddler in South Street hammered the balls all round with the sharp edge of his hammer, and the question of flight was solved. They no longer ducked in flight. Later, moulded markings were deliberately introduced to the new gutta ball which was made in various sizes and weights. Within a year or two, 'featheries' were museum pieces.

Not for forty years did the boy Paterson learn of the success of his venture and its happy repercussions for St. Andrews. The fateful interview with Allan Robertson and Morris took place on the eve of his departure for the U.S to a life that knew nothing of golf. He became the Rev. Dr Robert Adam Paterson who founded the first American Bible College for training women missionaries.

A canny Scots postscript: Gourlay, the noted ball-maker at Musselburgh, had a steady order for 'featheries' from Sir David Baird, a 'keen hand' as addicts were then known. He saw the gutta in action and his own re-action was prompt. He dispatched his full output of six dozen feather balls to his client. Sir David was one of the last players to adopt the gutta at St. Andrews!

An immediate repercussion of the gutta's advent was to open up the game to the artisans and the peasantry in larger numbers. The caddies and professionals long since had begun to ape their masters, and to better their betters with club and ball. Allan Robertson was invincible. From these tradesmen ranks came a steady stream of improving golfers who began to copy the gentlemen players in another respect . . . to form their own golf clubs and even clubhouses.

The coming of the railway line to nearby Leuchars attracted more visitors; some built houses and in 1850 exercised their influence to bring the railway to St. Andrews itself. Events were conspiring to help the town to a new prosperity and a new fame.

TIME-HONOURED CRAFT

ONE way in which events brought prosperity was the expansion in local clubmaking. Just as the game of golf is centuries old in St. Andrews, so, naturally, were the twin crafts of making its implements . . . the clubs and the balls. One of the earliest known manufacturers of both was James Pett, who, in 1672, was supplying the historically famous Marquis of Montrose. It was a full-time occupation for him. Henry Mill, about 1714, was also fully employed attending to the needs of golfers, and when David Dick of College Wynd died in 1731, leaving an orphan daughter, his trade was given as a clubmaker. (This information is contained in a legal document uncovered during the compiling of this volume. The purpose of the document was "serving and cognising as nearest and lawfull heir to her deceased grandfather, Robert Dick, burgess in the city, Lilias Dick, the daughter and only child of the deceased, David Dick, clubmaker in St. Andrews.")

Light is thrown on the trade at the time by the letter written by Professor Alexander Munro, a Regent of the University of St. Andrews to his friend, John Mackenzie of that ilk, a Principal Clerk of Session from 1688 to 1718, dated 27th April, 1691.

"Sir, Receive from the bearer, our post, ane sett of Golfe-Clubs, consisting of three, viz.: ane play-club, ane scraper and ane tin-faced club. I might have made the set to consist of more, but I know not of your play, and if you stand in need of more I think you should call for them from me. Tho I know you may be served there, yet I presumed that such a present from this place, the Metropolis of Golfing may not be unsuitable for these fields, especially when its come from a friend. Upon the same consideration I have also sent you ane dozen Golfe balls, which receive with the clubs. I am told they are good, but will prove according to your play and the fields. If the size do not suit, were you so free with me, I would mend it with the next. I am glad to have an occasion, and subscribe my selfe, still your faithful and most humble servant, Al. Munro."

"P.S. The bearer may have other clubs and balls from this place, but yours cannot be mistaken if you received them marked, viz.: the clubs with the letters G.M. as the tradesman's proper signe for himselfe, and J.M.K. for your mark stamped upon ilke ane of them. The balls are marked W.B., which are not ordinarily counterfeited."

Munro's friend, John Mackenzie, later sent his twin sons, Kenneth and Thomas to St. Andrews University with a tutor, one James Morice. The twins were allowed to play golf twice a week, when the weather was fair, the game being considered 'a diversion'. While at St. Andrews, Morice paid four shillings (Scots) for five balls in August, 1713, and the twins had ten balls at two shillings each. Kenneth also had a shaft and a club for four shillings.

One of the clubs which Munro himself owned is now in the possession of Laurie Auchterlonie, St. Andrews, the world expert on old golf clubs. One day, Laurie decided to strip the layers of oil from a club in his possession which he knew was very old. How old, he did not realise until he patiently uncovered the words, "Al. Munro, Aberdeen", and realised that the clubhead was one of Munro's own set *circa* 1700 when he held an appointment at Aberdeen University. A priceless collector's piece. It is a fair and reasonable assumption that earlier than the era of Henry Mill, the bowmakers were the makers of golf clubs as well—another early connection with archery.

The manufacture of golf clubs in St. Andrews reached its highest level possible with the materials then available in the early 1800s. Hugh Philp, a joiner and house painter by original trade, built up a clubmaking business by mending clubs for members. He became so adept that in September, 1819, he was appointed official clubmaker to the Society of Golfers and moved his premises from Argyle Street (just outside the West Port or city gate) down to more convenient premises beside the Union Parlour, the unofficial clubhouse of the members. From there, he moved to a building that was later occupied as the shop of Tom Morris.

Up to the time of Philp's appointment, the members of the Society, many of whom had town houses in Edinburgh, the capital city, had their equipment made by McEwan's of Musselburgh, who

Laurie Auchterlonie with his Priceless Munro Club (*circa* 1700)

Robert Forgan in his Cleek Factory, about 1880

practically monopolised the small general trade that there was in
Scotland at the time, succeeding Simon Cossar of Leith.

Peter MacEwan, who died in St. Andrews in 1971, represented the
sixth generation of MacEwans, the famous old clubmakers. He was
the last member of the oldest golfing family in the world, going back
to the early 1700s. Peter was a clubmaker and professional in various
parts of Scotland, although, as a firm, MacEwan's went out of
existence about 1880. Their clubs are now rare collectors' items.

The Society members from 1812, made increasing use of Philp's
conscientious services during their twice-yearly meetings in St.
Andrews, even although MacEwan's sent a representative to the
Autumn meetings. An intelligent craftsman, Philp was soon turning
out clubs that vied with the best in the country.

He became a master of his new craft, using thorn, apple, pear and
other indigenous hard woods. J. G. McPherson recalls:

> "With what affection did Allan (Robertson) look on his stock.
> The late Hugh Philp had polished at an apple tree head for a
> whole afternoon when modern makers would have considered it
> quite finished."

Hickory, the best wood for shafts, came later by chance with a
ballast cargo of that timber from Russia to Dundee. This was after
his nephew, Robert Forgan, had succeeded him in his business, on
Philp's death in 1856. Following its chance introduction, hickory
began to reach the Clyde in quantity from the famous Tennessee
hickory belt. On experimental try-out Forgan had found it ideal for
making shafts, with many virtues that other woods lacked.

From 1845 to 1852 Philp's chief assistant was James Wilson. In
that year Wilson set up for himself in a small shop on the site of
Rusack's Hotel which looks on the Links and for six years turned out
clubs that were the equal of Philp's best.

Because of the increasing use he made of the iron clubs of his day,
which were few, and were turned out by any available blacksmith to
the whims of any golfer, Allan Robertson also has the distinction of
really starting a new branch of the clubmaking industry . . . cleekmaking. Cleek was a general term used for any iron for many years,
the old Scots word meaning a hook. The original irons were for use

only when the ball lay so badly that to play it would endanger breaking a wooden club. Hence the name, track or rutting iron, with which the player "cleekit" or hooked the ball out of a rut.

Robertson became so skilful with the use of his 'cleek' for the unprecedented purpose of running-up from the fairway that he started a new fashion. The local blacksmiths were called upon to make iron clubs, and some of them, thanks to their craftsmanship and artistry (in the fashioning of ornamental iron gates, for instance) turned out excellent irons. Such blacksmiths as Robert Wilson, White and MacArthur, were highly recommended. "Few can beat them in the making of a fine, clean cleek" was a contemporary appreciation of their work.

The cleekmakers were an entirely separate and distinct branch of the trade for many years. They made irons; the clubmakers made woods, the only material originally used for all clubs.

Robert Wilson of North Street, in particular, brought refinement and grace to the shape of his iron heads which were made in an increasing range of elevations up to niblick. Previously they were coarse, heavy and clumsy weapons. His irons fully met the requirements of the somewhat unresilient gutta ball, and they became the model for later master-smiths. It was from this skill and initiative that the matched sets of today have evolved.

White, at the historic Cathedral Pends, the last user of water from the mediaeval mill lade before it was filled in, was another craftsman of the time. He was the first blacksmith to go over entirely to cleekmaking, and a notable apprentice to him was Tom Stewart who subsequently started his famous 'Pipe Brand' cleek factory in Argyle Street. Later, also, came Condie, of Market Street, and Anderson of nearby Anstruther, another artist in turning out iron heads. Down at the lifeboat station, Spence and Gourlay became the first cleekmakers to link up with a clubmaker when they joined Forgan, as recently as 1920. This was only a few years before the introduction of the steel shaft which revolutionised the industry.

Forgan, in clubmaking, introduced the method of driving in pegs to hold the bone to the soles of wooden clubs at a slant. He was succeeded by his son, Thomas, and during his time several innovations, such as the 'bulger' driver and Mellor's ebony putter were introduced. Thomas was father of the Forgan banking dynasty in the Middle West. His two banker sons who emigrated played a big part in popularising American golf.

In the early days of Philp a set of clubs would comprise a play-club or tee-club for driving, a long spoon, mid-spoon, short spoon, baffing spoon, driving putter and wooden putter. These were all wood. Also a sand iron or track or rutting iron. Later came the niblick of which Young Tom Morris became the acknowledged master. But Robertson was the originator of the short game with irons. As such, he revolutionised golf and the club making industry.

During Philp's lifetime the popularity of golf spread enormously in Scotland, both among the leisured classes and the artisans who lived near seaside Links. The trades of club- and cleekmaking expanded with it in St. Andrews and became a thriving local industry employing an increasing number of men. This continued throughout the 19th century and up to the mass-production days that followed the introduction of the steel shaft in Britain in 1929. Local clubmakers had been making them for export to the U.S. for five years before that date. Even in the thirties, clubmakers like Stewart, Condie, Anderson and Forgan, all since defunct, were famous for their products which went all over the world. Indeed, the world beat a track to the doors of the St. Andrews clubmakers.

It was a tragedy of economics that individuality had to give way to the production line. Stewarts, Forgans and the others died out or were swallowed up by big business, and then snuffed out.

Some sturdy individualists remain to whom the fashioning of a golf club is still an art. The greatest expert of them all is Laurie Auchterlonie. Although retired, he still "does enough to keep his hand in". Tom Auchterlonie does mostly running repairs and assembling, but he could, and still does, turn out a craftsman's article when required. Tom Morris is now almost entirely in the retail market. The Swilken Golf Company and the London-based Halley's manufacture their own clubs in premises in Largo Road for discerning home and overseas customers. Golf Classics, who moved into the Argyle Works in the late seventies, make wooden putters which, though based on the old and antique models, are practical working golf clubs.

It was from the shop of Tom Morris, run nowadays by Morris

Anderson, a member of another old clubmaking family and a clubmaker all his life, that the first clubs went to America. They were for the famous Apple-Tree gang of the St. Andrews Golf Club of Yonkers, the original golf club in the United States. Similarly Westward Ho, the first English seaside course, has a strong affiliation with this shop which sent the club's first equipment.

General Moncrieffe, an R. and A. member, went from St. Andrews to stay with his cousin, Mr Gossett, the Vicar of Northam. He was taken by his host for a walk across the Burrows to the Pebble Ridge, and exclaimed ecstatically, "Providence obviously designed this for a golf course!" And so Westward Ho, one of the earliest English courses, came into being soon after.

Laurie Auchterlonie, son of Willie, the last St. Andrews-based professional to win the Open, succeeded his father in 1964 as honorary professional of the Royal and Ancient Club, and runs the firm established by his father. He is the recognised expert on old clubs and balls, and is an honorary member of the American Hall of Fame Association, having supervised the setting up of their museum in Foxburg. He fits a set of clubs to the physical build of the player as a tailor does a suit. Laurie, in 1967, gave Gene Sarazen and Jimmy Demaret the thrill of a lifetime. He fitted them out with 50-year-old hickory clubs and one or two gutta balls and let them loose on the Old Course. Both returned with a new admiration for their pioneer professional predecessors! He was appointed, in 1972, honorary curator of the Pinehurst Golf Museum, U.S.A.

Today a Philp club is a museum piece. His success as a clubmaker, plus the advent of the gutta ball costing only a quarter of the 'featherie' and lasting much better, had the one highly important side effect on St. Andrews. It made golf available to greater numbers of the artisan or tradesman class of player. From these ranks there emerged soon after the professionals and greenkeepers of the game who spread golf over the world.

A HUNDRED YEARS' WAR

SCOTTISH lawyers have a soft spot for St. Andrews, not only for its golf, but professionally. It has the reputation with them of being a keenly litigious little city. The inhabitants perennially have been unable to resist that beloved requisite of the Scottish legal profession, "a guid gangin' plea", or lawsuit.

Towards the end of the 18th century the old town was plunging inexorably towards the nadir of a two hundred years' slide.

In 1769 Mr James Lumsden, then the laird of Strathtyrum, exchanged land with the Town Council by a deed of excambion. It was a deal that was notable because this was the first time in trans-actions between the Town Council and Strathtyrum that the condition was specific that the part of the Links then used for golf must be kept entire. It was as much due to Mr Lumsden as to the Council of the time that the agreement then signed preserved the golf course. He himself was a golfer.

The rights of playing could easily have been lost altogether at that time, and the history of St. Andrews entirely changed for the worst, but for that important clause.

Still later, the Town Council, administrators of the town's affairs, were heavily in debt, and felt they had no option other than to sell the ancient birthright of the citizens, the Links of St. Andrews and Pilmuir. The sale was the sequel originally of a mortgage which the Town was unable to fulfil.

This was negotiated in 1797 to Mr Thomas Erskine, later the Earl of Kellie. The sum paid was £805, but the ancient ecclesiastical and royal titles held by the city ensured that the ground could only change hands subject to the rights of the citizens to play golf at all times being guaranteed.

The sale of the Links, with such conditions attached, was considered highly questionable legally, and it was bound to lead to legal trouble. This soon followed. Erskine feued, or rented, the Links to Charles and Cathcart Dempster to use them for the purpose of breeding rabbits extensively. Nothing was more calculated to ruin the Links for golf than rabbit scrapes. Burrows soon began to play havoc with the Old Course!

The Royal and Ancient Golf Club, then still styled the Society of Gentlemen Golfers, complained loud and bitterly. The members even had to depart from their cherished basic principle of playing 'the ball where it lies' by introducing a temporary rule of lifting out of rabbit holes! This showed the measure of their deep concern.

Finally, the Society invoked the law to halt the rabbit pest, and the Hundred Years' War was on! A succession of lawsuits only ended a century later when the Town was able to buy back the part of the Links containing the Old Course. A special Parliamentary Act in 1894 re-established all their rights and privileges in regaining ownership . . . rights which they had managed to enjoy despite all attempts to filch them.

Paradoxically, those hundred years when the Links were out of the Town's possession spanned the golden era of St. Andrews golf. It was an era that brought new-found fame and fortune to the little city. Those years witnessed the local pastime of a handful of people expand, first into a national game, and then to an international sport and into big business as St. Andrews men spread golf across the world. They saw rules formed and tightened; the equipment for playing improved out of all recognition; the Old Course manicured and barbered out of its natural state of barren 'Links' into a sophisticated circuit expressly designed to ease and make more enjoyable the playing of golf . . . into golf as it is today.

Every significant step in the evolution of the game up to the invention of the rubber-cored ball originated in St. Andrews, and most of them were taken in that eventful century of years.

A long succession of lawsuits and counter-suits was required to decide finally the 'Rabbits Case' and later attempted infringements of the citizens' rights. Throughout, and unswervingly, the Scottish Law Courts have held that the right of the citizens and others to play golf over the Links is inviolate.

A judgement of Solomon settled the rabbits' issue. The Dempster family were legally informed they were entitled to continue to rear their rabbits on the Links, but should any of them stray on to that area known as the golf course, they could be killed as pests. (The course was a small, clear part in the centre of the whole Links.)

The unlucky Dempsters took out an injunction against the Town Council forbidding them "from assembling all and sundry by tuck of drum (the traditional form of public announcement) to proceed in a body to kill or expel the rabbits."

Not surprisingly, that is just what happened. An infuriated mob of town golfers invaded the Links and shot, snared and hunted the rabbits wholesale. Lawlessness on both sides followed, with the Dempsters fighting a losing battle, even when the rabbits could not multiply fast enough to beat the pogrom. In 1806, the Court, "with great unanimity", gave judgement in favour of the "Society" with expenses.

Appeals followed to the highest courts in the land over a period of fully ten years. By 1817 the Dempsters had given up the fight; the golfers, temporarily, had no more cause for complaint, and the town regained full possession of its birthright. But not for long.

In the fateful year for St. Andrews of 1848, the town was to all intents and purposes bankrupt. In their desperate financial straits the city councillors had sold more of the Links and other surrounding lands to Mr George Cheape, now laird of the neighbouring Strathtyrum, and a prominent member of the Society of Golfers. They received £5,683. The area containing the Old Course fetched £1,805, and the Council was able to repay part of its crippling debt of £10,000.

Again, a clear condition was conveyed in the sale that golf must continue as a free right. Mr Cheape, as Captain at this time of the Society, was himself anxious to ensure that.

The 'free' right is important. From time immemorial, until 1913, everyone, resident or visitor, golfed without charge at St. Andrews. From that date until 1946, the inhabitants only played free and without fee of any kind.

So, 1848 was the city's darkest hour. More lawsuits surrounding the golf course interspersed and enlivened the subsequent years. In 1859 rabbit scrapes were still plentiful and the R. and A. had recourse to the Court of Session who granted interdict to prevent rabbits from being allowed to burrow on the 'green'. An important suit was in 1874 when the Town Council themselves sought to deprive the citizens they represented of part of their ancient rights, by attempting to nibble at part of the 18th fairway for building purposes. The law courts refused permission.

The Royal and Ancient had to spring to their own defence and that of the townspeople. The Court sternly warned the city's councillors that they, more than anyone else, had no right "to encroach or to authorise any encroachment on the Links so as to diminish the area for the playing of golf."

Nothing emphasises more clearly than this pronouncement the clear character of the citizens' rights in the Links. The right of playing golf was absolute, as it still is today. Thus is explained the need for all the subsequent Acts of Parliament and Provisional Orders up to the present day whenever those rights become involved.

Some twenty years after 1874 came another crucial stage in the history of the Old Course. The Laird of Strathtyrum was persuaded in 1893 by the R. and A. to sell the Links to them for £5,000.

The game had burgeoned in popularity to such an extent that the members were in danger of being crowded off the golf course they had largely fashioned and maintained by other golfers playing free!

The Club wanted to construct a new course, doing away with the homeward holes of the Old Course. The members considered the High Hole unsafe, with its crossfire of golf balls and the serious congestion it entailed. Again, of course, this sale was subject to the rights of the citizens being assured.

Feeling rose high in St. Andrews when the position became public. The now-prosperous city, in its re-discovered pride, demanded the opportunity of buying back its ancient heritage. Appeal was made to Parliament.

With the tact and diplomacy that have always characterised their often difficult relations with the townspeople, the R. and A. gracefully withdrew. So, once again, in 1894, and after a century, St. Andrews came into full possession of its Old Course.

The Royal and Ancient Club was satisfied that the 1894 agreement secured it a permanent position and a considerable extension of golfing facilities to the members. One of the conditions laid down in the Act was the formation of a joint Green Committee, consisting of five members of the Club and two nominees of the Town Council, which would have sole charge of the management of the Links.

The R. and A. were compelled, at their own expense, to maintain the Old Course and also maintain the Ladies' Course (a putting green), for their exclusive use at a reasonable rent. The Old Course must always be open to members of the public. The same conditions applied to the New Course that the R. and A. were permitted to construct, except in July, August and September when payment was exacted on everyone except the R. and A. members, ratepayers of St. Andrews and the family and guests of the proprietors of Strathtyrum.

The clause in the 1894 Act imposing a charge on anyone to play golf in St. Andrews, was unprecedented in the Town's history. But the Old Course continued to be open for anyone to play free over its venerable turf for many more years.

Further legal sanctions have been necessitated since then, right up to the present day, by the steadily expanding popularity of the game.

By 1913, however, the intolerable congestion on both courses demanded drastic action. A fourth circuit, the Eden Course, was laid out south of the Old and immediately became a popular course for holiday golfers. On it the 'Eden' Tournament, the largest amateur event in Britain, with entries averaging 300, has been played since. At the same time the local authorities agreed that free golf for visitors must go. Charges were imposed for all courses, the most revolutionary step being a tariff on the hitherto free Old Course. Only residents and the R. and A. could play there without charge!

A nine-hole course for children — Balgove Links — was laid out in 1972.

Further recourse to the law courts was needed in 1932 to allow still more impositions to be made. These included an admission charge on all spectators who wanted to watch championship events being played on the Links! Before then, there had been no restriction to prevent anyone from walking freely all over the Links, even when the Open Championship was being played!

Final shattering of the age-old tradition of free golf came when the townspeople, in 1946, were charged up to a maximum of £2 per year for playing golf on their own courses.

Never before, in the age-long history of the Old Course, had they paid for their golf. This measure required a new Parliamentary Order which was preceded by a lengthy and exhaustive public inquiry at Edinburgh.

Sunday golf on the other three courses, including the Jubilee, remodelled by Willie Auchterlonie during the last war, has only been permitted since 1941, first as a wartime concession, and after the war, in deference to insistent demand.

The ruling at that time met stern opposition from local Sabbatarians and was also bitterly opposed on the grounds of the dictum of old Tom Morris that "the course needs a rest on Sundays if the players don't". The advent of the Second World War hastened on the reluctant acceptance of Sunday golf in St. Andrews rather more quickly than would otherwise have been the case. It established the precedent.

LOCAL CLUBS EMERGE

SIGNIFICANT expansion of the purely localised club-making industry that was then at least 300 years old in St. Andrews began around the year 1800, when the members of the Society of Golfers increasingly made use of the local services in preference to Musselburgh and Edinburgh. This factor had the tremendously important effect of encouraging many more St. Andrews artisans and shop-keepers to take up the game. It fostered the latent love of the town's traditional game in the tradesmen actually working at clubmaking, and they communicated the fever, never long quiescent, to their fellow tradesmen and others.

The equipment became more easily and cheaply available to them, and when the gutta arrived on the scene in 1848 its cost was only a quarter of the 'featherie', while it also lasted much longer. Golf was now within the purse of the working man!

The artisans began also to emulate the aristocratic societies in playing competitive matches. Working hours were long and arduous for most of them, but in the long summer evenings and also in the early dawning they golfed. As their numbers swelled, the ambition also arose in them to form their own societies, even to acquire premises. For their part, the gentlemen of the Society were pleased to encourage the lower classes in their 'healthful exercise', often with the help of their own discard equipment and second- and third-hand 'featheries' and, later, guttas.

This highly important development was to climax in the emergence of the young Allan Robertson, who had worked hard at this game which the gentlemen played. From his earliest days Robertson spent most of his few leisure hours on the Old Course, and there the grey dawn of four o'clock of a high summer morning would usually find him, by no means always alone, snatching early holes before the Society members were astir and with a long day's work ahead of him.

By the time that the gutta ball had come on the scene, conditions were ripe for the golden era of golf – the years that raised it from an obscure local pastime to its international pre-eminence. The intelligent artisans, like Hugh Philp, became craftsmen in making clubs or professionals in the skills of the game itself. The workshys and unemployables found a pleasant way round work in caddying to the Gentlemen. To them it was a congenial form of labour, because of their vicarious enjoyment gained through participation in their 'man's' game, as his club-carrier.

In 1817 the Thistle Club for merchants and tradesmen of the town was the first local golf organisation to be formed. It continued until 1838, faded out, but returned to the golfing scene in 1865, and still flourishes today, an organisation without premises.

Entirely different is the history of the St. Andrews Golf Club which began life as the Mechanics' Club in September, 1843.

The St. Andrews Club, as already emphasised, must not be confused by the visitor to the city with the Royal and Ancient Club, although next to that august institution, it has the most illustrious history of any golf club in the world. It prospered from the start, the name being changed from the 'Mechanics' in 1851 to the present more general title. For long it has been the largest as well as the oldest artisan or tradesmen's club in the world. The annual subscription is probably still the smallest anywhere, despite the luxurious facilities the St. Andrews Club provides its members.

For many years the members were anxious to buy premises of their own, and attempts to procure property were made as early as 1851. In conjunction with other local clubs, they tried at a later date to secure a site for a joint clubhouse on the Bruce Embankment, without success.

A building fund was steadily accumulating over the years, but it was as late as 1905 before the Club managed to buy a house at the corner of Golf Place, one hundred yards from the Home Green. The Royal and Ancient Club gave them a donation towards expenses of £50. A bazaar raised £450 in two days! – A huge sum in those days.

At the first foregathering in their new home the members made townsman Sandy Herd, winner of the 1902 Open, an honorary member. Then, in 1933, the present spacious and excellently situated premises were secured. They have been converted into a clubhouse that contains every amenity a golfer could wish for. The Scottish tradition, infrangible in the R. and A., of barring ladies from the premises has been only slightly relaxed in the case of the St. Andrews Club. The women golfers of the town possess their own clubhouses, but have entry to one lounge of the men's club.

No more glittering honours board will be found in the world for the members of an individual club. Its crowded lists include in addition to numerous minor honours, the names of members, as winners of 19 Open Championships, three American Opens, two Amateur Opens, one American Open Amateur . . . a dazzling international array. In 1898 Fred Herd won the U.S. Open and Finlay Douglas the U.S. Amateur – an international clean sweep by St. Andrews Club members.

Captains of the Club have included, appropriately, the first professional, Allan Robertson, whose locker is traditionally used by reigning captains. Members of golfing families of St. Andrews fame, such as four generations of Aytons, have been associated with it since its foundation. Innumerable members of the St. Andrews Club have gone all over the world in the last hundred years, teaching the game they learned on the Old Course from their ancestors.

A remarkable tradition of the St. Andrews Club is the two fifty-a-side matches played every year on a home-and-away basis. One, against Leven Thistle some dozen miles away, began in 1849, three years after that club was founded; and the Carnoustie match in 1873. They play nowadays for the Lindsay Trophy, presented in memory of J. L. Lindsay, a brilliant St. Andrews amateur of the 1940s.

Another tradition is the annual New Year's Day competition, first established in 1873. New Year is the ancient Scottish holiday, and St. Andrews men could and still conceive no better way of starting the year than with a competitive round of golf. Postponement because of the weather has been remarkably infrequent, thanks to the mild, insular climate.

Of the many trophies played for, the gold medal presented by the Royal and Ancient Club for the stroke play championship of the St. Andrews Links, and the F. G. Tait Memorial Medal for match play, are the most treasured. "Freddie" Tait, an R. and A. member killed in the Boer War in 1900, is one of the few St. Andrews golfing heroes who earned that special niche in their hearts amounting to hero-worship.

Another club 'first' was the founding of the earliest University Golf Club in 1853, and a long line of notable players has been produced from students who had their initiation to golf when they came to St. Andrews to pursue their academic studies.

A Madras College Club, then a boarding school, was in existence in 1857. It is recorded that in May of that year a pupil, Robert Ross, a member of the School Club, went round in 93. Allan Robertson presented a Duke of Wellington Medal to the club for a competition under handicap. One of the boys, James Kirk, playing from the handicap of scratch, won it after a tie with Alex Strath. Both were notable family names in St. Andrews golf.

The first organisation of women golfers in the world was the St. Andrews Ladies' Club, born in 1867, of which the comment was written a year or two later:

> "Born in the soil of St. Andrews Links, and making a struggle for existence and for recognition, its remarkable success has led to the introduction of the culture of golf as a family recreation in England and elsewhere . . . of course, the wielding of the club assumes a mild form under the sway of the gentler sex, and has never as yet extended beyond the simple strokes of the putting green."

The state of ladies' golf as a "mild form" did not last long! Out of the Club which still functions, developed the St. Rule Ladies' Club, and by 1893 the first Ladies' Championship had taken place.

The women's game was revolutionised by the Hezlet sisters. Then the sisters Cecil and Edith Leitch introduced a new standard of play when they appeared in the 1908 championship on the Old Course. Daughters of a Fife man, they learned their golf at Silloth. They entered unknown but by the end of the week in the Championship they had become national figures and future champions.

Following on the opening of the New Course in 1895, traffic on the Links continued to rocket to an unprecedented extent. Business people in the city felt that still another clubhouse was needed because of the swelling tide of annual visitors attracted by golf. In 1902 the New Club was formed, with premises in Links Road, bordering the last fairway of the Old Course. From its inception it became a vital and vigorous institution, and in its relatively short existence it has built up a record of golf honours equal to that of many older clubs. Like the St. Andrews Club, it boasts a membership of over 1,700, with a modest subscription for the facilities provided. About forty per cent of the membership are country members and visitors. "Semper Nova", the whimsical club motto, was adopted recently, and ladies are admitted to its enlarged premises.

In the 1894 legal proceedings, the membership of the St. Andrews Club was given as 84; and the Thistle Club 60, the University Club 47, and the Guild Club 26 — a total of 217 local golfers in all. The Royal and Ancient Club membership was then 909. These figures demonstrate strikingly the rocketing upsurge between then and now in the popularity of golf.

Most recent in origin of the St. Andrews clubs is the St. Regulus Ladies' Club, which has already celebrated its half-century.

THE FIRST PROFESSIONALS

ALLAN ROBERTSON, to whom frequent reference has been made in these pages, was the first professional golfer in the world. He was born into what was the oldest-known golfing family in St. Andrews, traditional golf ball makers for generations. His father and grandfather before him had been caddies, and his father, "Davie", was the senior caddie of those who served the Royal and Ancient Club . . . "Davie, oldest of the cads", he was described in George Fullarton Carnegie's "Golfiana", written about 1830. As with a few before him, and many since, Allan was born almost with a club in his hand.

In addition to becoming the 'best golfer in the world', he was also largely responsible for early improvements to the condition of the Old Course as well as the general standard of play. He was the first real professional. Although never attached formally to the R. and A. he was backed by the members in most of his challenge matches. At his death in 1859, one biographer claimed of him that he was 'the greatest golf-player that ever lived, of whom alone it can be said that he was never beaten'. The claim is not as extravagant as it sounds today, since before Robertson any records were inaccurate, and he was outstanding in his time. A record of his money matches from 1840 to the year of his death confirms the claim that in that sphere he was never beaten. Although defeated in rare single-round contests, he did not once lose a full match, generally played over a stated number of rounds.

The biggest money game of last century took place as early as 1849 when Robertson and Tom Morris played a challenge match against the two Dunns of Musselburgh for £400. That was very big money in those days. As comparison, fifty years later the prize for winning the Open was still under £50! Members of the R. and A. were never slow at putting up money to "back their fancies".

Victory went to the St. Andrews pair by two holes, after rounds at Musselburgh, St. Andrews and North Berwick. At one stage they were 13 holes down, but eventually won by an aggregate of two holes over the series, finishing at North Berwick.

Allan Robertson, World's First Professional

Andra Kirkaldy, Last of an Era

"Thus they won the match, one of the most brilliant and extraordinary in the whole annals of golfing" ran the report.

Earlier, in 1843, Allan won a match of twenty rounds, lasting ten days, over the Old Course, against Willie Dunn of Musselburgh. He won on the last day by being two rounds to the good, with one round or 18 holes to play. A few months before his death at the age of 44 years he became the first man in the world to break eighty, with a round of 79 over the Old Course in a friendly match with Mr Bethune of Blebo, a member of the Society of St. Andrews Golfers. He was described by a contemporary biographer as "a short, little, active man, with a pleasant face and a merry twinkle in his eye. His style was neat and effective and he held his clubs near the end of the handle, even his putter high up. With him the game was one of head as much as hand; he always kept cool, and generally pulled through a match, even when he got behind. He was a natural gentleman."

His great partner, Tom Morris, who outlived him by so long, described Allan as 'the cunningest bit body o' a player that ever handled club, cleek or putter'. This was an assessment made many years later after a wide experience of the best in amateur and professional golf over a lengthy period. His pitching was deadly!

Part of Allan's Celtic whimsy, which also inspired a tendency to practical joking and 'leg-pulling', was to give a name to every club in his bag. Each had a distinct personality to him and he started a habit that many famous golfers have subsequently followed as, for instance, Bobby Jones with his Calamity Jane. Allan's short game clubs were "Sir David Baird" (a prominent R. and A. member), "The Doctor", "Sir Robert Peel" (politician), "Thraw-cruik" (wry-neck) and "The Frying Pan" (his favourite iron).

A memorial in honour of his many distinguished achievements, erected by public subscription, can be seen in the old Town Cemetery, the last resting place also of the Morrises, father and son, and a shrine of golfing history.

By far the best-known Scottish figure in the emergent days of golf was Old Tom Morris whose 87 years of life spanning from 1821 to 1908, mark the most vital epoch in the game and the golden era for St. Andrews. Like Robertson, he was of old St. Andrews stock. Appointed greenkeeper to the Royal and Ancient Club in 1865, after having been enticed to Prestwick for about fourteen years, he saw and played a big part in the astounding spread of golf over the world. As St. Andrews became increasingly a Mecca of golfers, so too did the sturdy patriarchal figure and bearing of Old Tom come to symbolise all that was finest in the Scottish character and in the ancient Scottish game. His kindly, yet capable and gentle nature enshrined him a good many years before his death as the authentic Grand Old Man of Golf. To generations of people all over the world his name and his picture epitomised golf.

As a player himself, he never earned the fame that was Allan Robertson's before him, yet Tom Morris was four times Open Champion and had, on occasion, beaten Robertson.

It was the combination of respect and affection with which he came to be held by the members of the Royal and Ancient Club, whose first professional he was, and by all who came in contact with him, that he is best remembered. The famous and unknown alike, of the world's golfers coming to St. Andrews, he had the gift of making feel at home on his Old Course. He watched over its maintenance with an undeviating vigilance, and had two strict rules for its care. The first, simply, was 'mair saund, Honeyman' . . . the constant application of sharp, sea sand to the greens and fairways to maintain the character of the turf. Honeyman was for long his sole assistant. The second. 'Nae Sunday play. The course needs a rest if the gowfers don't'.

This latter dictum came to be so traditionally accepted that the Clerk to the Joint Links Committee was surprised to find when the question of Sunday play arose, that the records contained no legal ban against the Old Course being open to Sunday play.

When the first patent hole-cutter was invented about 1869 by Charles Anderson, Fettykil, he presented it as a tribute to Morris.

Old Tom competed in every Open Championship up to, and including, 1896, a period of 36 years in all. He was greenkeeper in charge of the Old Course until 1904 when he retired at the age of 83 years. The measure of the respect and affection he commanded was that he was immediately elected honorary professional of the Royal and Ancient Golf Club. His portrait in oil hangs in a prominent place in the Clubhouse, while the Home Green was named the Tom Morris Green in his memory.

To compare the 'greats' of different generations in any sport is a pointless task. In the case of 'Young Tom', the son of Tom Morris, it is completely futile. Where hundreds played then, millions today throng the courses of the world. Since his day, course maintenance and implements have improved tremendously, making it a different game.

Suffice to leave it that 'Young Tom' was peerless in his day.

Born in St. Andrews, he spent the first 14 years of his life at Prestwick where his father was greenkeeper. They returned to St. Andrews in 1864 and almost immediately the boy began to demonstrate an amazing aptitude for the game. At Carnoustie, in 1867, at the age of 16 years he beat all comers, including the great Willie Park of Musselburgh. He also won the Open Professional Tournament at Montrose against the best in the land, among them his father. Then he won an individual challenge match against Park. From then on, Young Tom was unbeatable. He won the Open Championship Belt in the following year, and by 1870 had annexed it three years in a row, to make it his own personal property.

In his invaluable book of the period, "Golf" Robert Clark, himself a fine player, records:

> "So the trophy, which consists of red morocco and is an exquisite piece of workmanship, richly ornamented with massive silver plates bearing appropriate devices, and produced at a cost of thirty guineas, becomes the property of 'Young Tom'".

It is now a prized possession of the Royal and Ancient Golf Club whose members purchased it from the Morris family in 1938.

After the interval of a year when no championship was played, a new Challenge Cup was subscribed for, to replace the Belt, to be played for annually on the three greens of Prestwick, St. Andrews and Musselburgh. In its first year, Tommy was again victorious, with a score of 160, giving him the distinction of being the champion in four successive years.

More impressive by far than the actual victories of this remarkable prodigy was the wide margin of his wins. He won by 11 strokes over 36 holes in 1869, and by 12 shots in the following year. His winning aggregates were: 1868, 154; 1869, 157; 1870, 149; 1872, 160. His average of 74½ in 1870 was unbeaten while the contest remained over 36 holes, which was until 1891. At his peak he was described as having no weakness in any department of his game. He was gifted with unusual physical strength, allied to the true champion's concentration and determination to win.

A description of his swing given in a contemporary account of a match was "that he scorned the typical full, easy St. Andrews style of striking". With a shorter swing than average, he punched the ball rather after the present-day American method. In 1869 he broke the record for the Old Course of 79 set up by Allan Robertson twelve years before, with a score of 77. This was against Bob Ferguson in a money match.

James Wolfe Murray, scion of a noble family and a member of the R. and A. who seemed to have a penchant for the unusual, challenged Young Tom with bow-and-arrow. A skilled archer, he finished the winner, but only narrowly.

Young Tom was a handsome, friendly lad who had much of his father's geniality. He was the idol of golfing Scotland when he died at the untimely age of 24 years. The handsome memorial stone to his memory in the Old Town Churchyard, was subscribed for by golfers and clubs all over the country.

In October 1973 there was an unusual one-man celebration of a centenary. Jim Kidd flew to St. Andrews from Montreal to celebrate the centenary of the 1873 Open Championship. His great-grandfather won the Open in 1873 — the first year that great event was ever staged at St. Andrews — and in so doing halted the sequence of four wins in a row by Young Tommy Morris. Tom Kidd's aggregate for the 36 holes was 179, and Jim Kidd's object was to go round in fewer strokes than his illustrious forebear. Jim, who was 39 years of age at the time, scored 107 for his first round and 95 for his second — a total of 202, failing by a pretty wide margin. But he was not despondent. He said afterwards — "I shall have another go at beating Tom's score. I was getting to know the course all the time, and getting better. If I played the course more often, I feel I could get into the eighties."

HONOUR WITHOUT REWARD

THE step-up from caddie to a new and higher rank of professional golfer, first made by Allan Robertson, was not a very high one, either financially or socially. Honours and adulation were gained in plenty by Robertson, but the reward of hard cash still lay in the years far ahead of his time.

For over 60 years from 1850 a livelihood, often a precarious one at that, was all the professional could expect to get out of golf, apart from his love for the game. St. Andrews reared a successive crop of Open champions, but none of them died rich. The chance of a little more money than a tradesman could earn at his job, and slightly more congenial living conditions was as much as they could hope for. Young Tom Morris was tempted to cross the Border by the promise of good rewards, but his father thought he was too young. Many others, later on, did leave their native town for England and much farther afield, but only because their conditions and prospects were so poor at home.

Perhaps the unluckiest golfer of the early professional era was Davie Strath, boon friend of Young Tom, but overshadowed by him. He was one of two golfing brothers born in St. Andrews. His brother Andrew won the Open in 1865 at the age of 19, but Davie was considered the better player, probably because of his effortless style, with its typically smooth and fluent St. Andrews swing. He was unlucky, too, in actual play on at least one notable occasion due to the casual nature of the championship arrangements of the time. Davie had the 1876 Open in his pocket. It was played over the Old Course, and at the Long Hole in, on his second round, his drive felled another St. Andrews player, a non-competitor having a friendly round on the course! The incident upset Strath more than it did his victim and he dropped shots to tie with Bob Martin, a fellow St. Andrean. Then also, at the Road Hole, the 17th, he was involved in an incident. Galleries were more partisan in those early days before the R. and A. took over the championship arrangements and imposed their own strict code on the spectators—a code of impartiality that is part of the St. Andrews tradition. Some of

Martin's supporters claimed Strath should be disqualified for playing to the green before the match ahead had left it.

But this was probably the worst managed Open Championship in history, and the committee could not decide whether to sustain the complaint or not. They decreed a play-off, but the incensed Strath refused to appear, and Martin was awarded the title, with Strath getting £5 as runner-up. He removed soon after to North Berwick, became ill and died on a health voyage to Australia, aged 39.

His brother Andrew went to Prestwick as greenkeeper, and was an excellent club and ball maker, but he also died young, at the age of 32. A third brother, George, was no great player, but was an excellent teacher as he proved when he went to Troon to become their first professional. George was probably also the first 'pro' to emigrate to America, primarily as a golfer — the beginning of a new era!

It was a tragic coincidence that three of the town's foremost golfers, Morris and the two Straths, should all die so young. The Strath memorial is the deadly little hazard guarding the right hand side of the 11th green . . . Strath Bunker, the graveyard of many golfing hopes.

Willie Fernie, born in the same year as Young Tom, developed much later as a player and he did not win an Open Championship until 1883, after being second in the previous year to Bob Ferguson of Musselburgh. He left St. Andrews in 1880 and was greenkeeper at Dumfries, Felixstowe and Ardeer before going to Troon. He played in many of the big wager matches of the time, including two against the redoubtable and intimidatory Andrew Kirkaldy, both of which he won. Fernie represented Scotland at the advanced age of 53 against England in 1904, and for years was in great demand as a teacher. He was also one of a unique triumvirate of St. Andrews men to win the Open Championship in this period. The other two were Jack Burns and Sandy Herd. All were staunch members of the St. Andrews Club.

They were typical of these hard pioneering days of professional golf. All of them served apprenticeships as plasterers in the tiny yard of Andrew Scott in South Street — undoubtedly the only tradesman's yard ever to produce three Open Golf champions! It stood about 100 yards inside West Port, the historic gateway landmark of the ancient ecclesiastical city, and on the south side of the street.

Rewards for tourneys were still microscopic. As example, Young Tom Morris won £6 with his first championship title, and £8 two years later. The canny St. Andrews golfers felt safer in face of such scant rewards with the security of a trade behind them to fall back on!

Tom Kidd, champion of 1873 – the first Open to be played on the Old Course – combined the duties of caddie, manservant and player. Bob Martin, for many years one of the best workmen in Old Tom's shop, between winning two Opens travelled to Cambridge to instruct the new University club there. Tom Kidd, incidentally, was the first man to "rib" an iron club to impart stop and it won him the 1873 Open, on bone-hard and lightning-fast St. Andrews greens. A century later, to the day, his great-grandson, Jim Kidd, from Canada, failed to beat his ancestor's Open winning score on a sentimental visit.

Positions as professionals and greenkeepers were not always even too secure. As late as 1888, after his Open win, Jack Burns went as professional to the recently-formed Warwick Club. Within a few years the former Champion was back at St. Andrews working as a platelayer on the railway line because 'he preferred a steady job'. In later years the linesman's favourite joke when asked about his golf exploits, was to reply: "I was never better. I have'na been aff the line for years." Burns established a record of 76 at Monifieth near Dundee that stood for 25 years.

So, while this was the golden era for the patrician R. and A. and the other old Societies, the golden years of professionalism still lay far ahead. Too far for St. Andrews winners of the Open Championship such as Tom Kidd, Bob Martin, Jamie Anderson, Hugh Kirkaldy, Willie Auchterlonie and Sandy Herd. So numerous were St. Andrews Open Champions at this time that on one occasion three turned out for the St. Andrews Golf Club in a married men's team against the club's bachelors!

Anderson won three Open Championships in all, and in consecutive years from 1877. He was noted for his steadiness, accuracy and coolness. At Prestwick, where he won in 1878, he teed-up to play the vital 17th. He was warned he could be disqualified if he played the ball from its position which was in front of the markers. Calmly Jamie replaced his ball, re-addressed it and holed out in one! Born at St. Andrews in 1842, he was the son of old 'Daw' Anderson, a caddie with some claim to fame himself as a 'character'. Jamie began to play golf at the age of ten years, and soon became known for his rifle-like straightness with every shot, his deadliness with his putter. He left St. Andrews for some time to become professional at Ardeer in the west of Scotland, but soon returned to his native town as player and clubmaker.

By 1890, St. Andrews professionals were eagerly heeding the advice of the early pioneers who had emigrated: "Go west, young man, go west!"

AMBASSADORS ABROAD

IT is a plain statement of fact that St. Andrews more than any other Scottish town spread golf across the globe.

Scottish ambition to 'get on in the world', spurred by the unpromising conditions and prospects at home, drove many families to emigrate from their country in the 19th century. For St. Andrews men, their knowledge of golf was sometimes the only asset they carried overseas, but it brought prosperity to most of them.

A steady stream of professionals and greenkeepers has left the old grey city for all parts of the world for more than 100 years. At first it was a slow and fearful trickle, but from 1880 onwards it became a steady and confident stream.

The earliest of the golfing emigrants was Davie Robertson, elder brother of the famous Allan. Davie decided in 1848, the year that produced the gutta ball, to try his luck in Australia. Once there, he introduced golf and was soon giving exhibitions all over the Colony where soon a number of courses of a kind were formed. He played a leading part in helping to form a body called the Australian Golf Society. It became the ruling body, headed for many years by another St. Andrews emigré.

Five years later Davie's brother Allan had become Captain of the local St. Andrews Golf Club and Davie sent home easily the most unusual golf prize up to that time, two nuggets of gold as prizes for a special competition to mark Allan's captaincy.

The initial link formed in Australia by Davie Robertson was cemented forty years afterwards by the later St. Andrews personality who settled "down under", became the father of golf administration there and a leading educationalist. He was Peter Corsar Anderson, student son of the Rev. Mark Anderson, of the Town Church, and winner of the 1893 Amateur Championship. Peter and J. Proudfoot were currently two of the best amateurs in the University Club. Being equally impecunious, they pooled their resources, then tossed for which should go to Prestwick for the event. Peter won the flip of the coin and went on to win the amateur title at the age of 21. For health reasons he travelled to Australia, but never used his return ticket. He died in 1955 at the age of eighty-two, honoured as the country's most distinguished golf administrator.

Other students of St. Andrews University played key parts in the international administration of golf as its popularity soared. Charles Blair Macdonald, son of a local emigrant to the United States, returned to St. Andrews to live with his grandfather while at University. The golf bug bit him badly and he rose to championship stature at St. Andrews. When he returned to America he was twice runner-up in the newly-promoted Amateur Championship before winning it in 1895. More important, as a member of the Royal and Ancient Club, he took a leading part in golf administration and advised on the setting up of the American Golf Association, particularly in connection with the rules. His liaison work between the American and British bodies over a number of years helped to establish a happy relationship of compromise between the two in a period of rapid change and conflicting ideas.

His work was recognised before he died when he was given the highest honour that American golf can bestow.

Yet, in his early days, Macdonald was not noted in America for his tact or diplomacy. He and John Reid, referred to below, were two of the founder members of the U.S. Amateur Golf Association. In 1892 he constructed at Chicago one of the first courses in America and his supreme architectural achievement was the "National Links of America", near Southampton, Long Island. For this, he copied many of the most famous holes in British golf, including the 11th and 17th of the Old Course. Macdonald was largely responsible for the first American contribution to the Rules of Golf. This was the out-of-bounds rule, later accepted by the Royal and Ancient Club. Until then, with St. Andrews, it was a basic principle that the ball must be played where it lay. Many a miraculous recovery had been played from the railway line, now disused, that bounds the 15th and 16th holes of the Old.

Contemporary with Macdonald, and making a vitally important contribution to golf in America were D. R. Forgan, author of the well-known "Philosophy of Golf", and his brother, J. B. Forgan. They were sons of Robert Forgan, the clubmaker, and they founded a banking dynasty in Chicago and district. David, in the early 'nineties, was working in a bank in Minneapolis, and after a visit home to St. Andrews returned with clubs and balls from his father's shop. He showed them to a friend, Jaffary, and they went to a farm that had some suitable grazing land, and golfed there, with trees as holes. This was the first of golf in Minnesota. Later the brothers had much to do with advancing the popularity of the game in the Chicago area and with the founding of the Washington Park Club there.

But of course, St. Andrews was closely concerned with the very beginning of golf in America. A tiny street near the city centre, Lockhart Place by name, bears testimony to the fact. It was built by the Lockhart family of Dunfermline linen fame, who holidayed regularly at St. Andrews for years, 'for the golf'.

One of them, Robert L. Lockhart, became his firm's American representative, and he took across the Atlantic with him in 1887 some Tom Morris golf clubs and two dozen balls for himself and John Reid, another ex-Dunfermline man. Reid was the founder of the famous Apple-Tree gang who, in 1888, formed the St. Andrews Club of Yonkers, the first American Golf Club.

Within the Royal and Ancient Clubhouse, presented to them by the Yonkers Club, reposes a branch of one of the apple trees mounted in silver. The trees were the feature of the first laid-out course, and gave the pioneer golfers their name.

Finlay Douglas was another St. Andrews student who made his mark on early American golf, particularly by many years in administration and also by winning their Amateur Championship in 1898. This was the year that his fellow-member of the St. Andrews Golf Club, Fred Herd, won the American Open – a St. Andrews double!

Douglas was runner-up in the subsequent two years when the title was won by that putting demon, Walter J. Travis, who was later to shock Britain to the core by winning our Amateur at Sandwich and starting the reverse process of American domination that continued so long. In 1959, shortly before his death, Douglas was awarded the Bobby Jones Trophy for distinguished service to golf.

The putting of Travis with his centre-shaft club left a tremendous impression on the golfing world. So much so that the St. Andrews cleekmakers were inundated with orders for the new type of putter. They went into full-scale production and had thousands made when it was announced that the R. and A. were not disposed to accept them as legal. The heads were dumped on the scrapheap a few months later in their thousands, amid the mutterings of many about the "reactionary" ruling body.

Numerous St. Andrews-born professionals have taken golf over the world and many still pepper the American golf scene. Special mention must be made of 'Jock' Hutchison. As a promising member of the local St. Andrews Golf Club, Jock heard the call of the West as a young man. He returned to his native St. Andrews a player improved out of all recognition in 1921, and an American citizen. As such, he took the Open Championship Cup back on the first of its many trips across the Atlantic after a replay with Roger Wethered, a noted amateur and subsequent captain of the R. and A.

'Jock' was a life-long member of his old club and a highly regarded honorary member. On his last visit 'home' as he still regarded St. Andrews, he was in his late seventies, but, as he told the writer, 'canna keep warm' in our stern climate. He, too, was signally honoured by and became a father figure in American Golf, while the members of his old club in St. Andrews play annually for the trophy he presented to them. He died in the United States in 1977, at the age of 93.

In his St. Andrews Open, Hutchison came within an inch of a unique championship feat. In one round he holed out in one at the 8th, and then drove the 9th green. The ball trickled up to the flag when an excited spectator rushed over, drew out the stick, and the ball rolled over the hole when it might have dropped at the flag for a second successive single! He was deadly with his irons throughout the event and three times hit the flag with full shots!

Less well-known and of the same vintage as Jock Hutchison was Harry Christie, who gave Walter Hagen his first lessons in golf. Walter never failed to look up Christie's relatives when in St. Andrews.

No personality in the golf world in America was more revered by St. Andreans at home and all over America than Jack Jolly who died in 1964. For years he made himself a reception committee of one to innumerable fellow-citizens at New York quayside and welcomed them to America, their new home. He was an unofficial home news agency, and a 'big brother' to many compatriots. He could always put any St. Andrean in the States in touch with another or with 'home'. He spent over 60 of his 80 years in the U.S. but St. Andrews was never out of his mind. Jack was a good player, but early went into the ball-making industry and it was in manufacture that he was chiefly concerned. He played in the 1902 American Open and saw his fellow townsman, Laurie Auchterlonie, uncle of the present 'Laurie', win it. The company of which he became president was the oldest ball manufacturing company in the States. Jack was deservedly made a life member of the U.S. Golf Association in 1961. For years he had been a life member of the St. Andrews Golf Club. The silver memorial trophy endowed by his family to the Club is outstandingly handsome.

Rather strangely, Ireland knew nothing of golf until 1884. It was introduced that year by the army. Brigadier General Sir David Kinloch of Gilmerton learned to golf at the nearby Old Course as a boy. In the Autumn of 1884 he was quartered with his regiment at Richmond Barracks, Dublin. Along with Mr John Oswald of Dunnikier, he laid out a few holes in Phoenix Park. The game caught on immediately and a small club was formed, the members including A. J. Balfour who became the father of English golf. The publicity his political fame brought to his favourite game south of the Scottish border was immense.

Golf arrived in Canada rather earlier than in the United States, but its progress was not so spectacularly rapid. The second club to be formed, that of the Quebec Club, was formally opened by Mrs Hunter, the daughter of Tom Morris, and her husband.

END OF AN ERA

PROBABLY the last survivor of the rugged old school of playing professionals before the emergence of the new, as typified by Walter Hagen, Henry Cotton and so on, was Andra Kirkaldy. During his time as honorary professional of the Royal and Ancient Club, golf reached a new summit of popularity in Britain with the wealthy and famous of the nation. They flocked to St. Andrews to golf on the Old Course, and deemed themselves lucky to gain Andra's attention; to squirm delightedly under the lash of his brusque tongue. Although the last of an era, he was regarded as the very epitome of the Scottish professional.

Yet Andra was the complete antithesis of Tom Morris, the genial and kindly honorary pro of the R. and A. whom he succeeded. Where Morris was urbane and natively polite, Kirkaldy was the roughest of rough diamonds. To many of his Club members he was the hairshirt of their self-esteem that the clown provided to the ancient royal courts. Of limited education, he had a brusque and ready tongue, although, no doubt, to many of his crushing ripostes have been added some that are apocryphal. He was no respecter of persons, and his language at times crude and unprintable. Perhaps the perfect example of his personality was provided by the incident when he was detailed by a Club member to meet two American friends making a special pilgrimage to the Mecca of Golf, and to give them a game.

Andra duly met the visitors at the railway station, brusquely greeted them; in complete silence he conducted them down to the clubhouse. He was awaiting them on the tee when they had changed for their round. Swiftly, Kirkaldy teed-up his ball, and sent a magnificent drive down the middle of the fairway.

Belligerently, he turned round to the two bewildered guests.

"Noo," he bellowed, "beat that, ye buggers!"

He is also recorded to be the original perpetrator of the old Scottish chestnut: "How's the world treating you these days, Andra?" "Verra seldom, sir. Verra seldom!"

Born at Denhead, on the outskirts of St. Andrews in 1860, Kirkaldy became a good golfer early on. In contrast to his brother, Hugh, whom he always claimed to be the better golfer, he had a beautiful, rhythmic swing. Seeing little future in golf, and with no other training, he joined the army, enlisting in the Highland Light Infantry at the age of 18. He served in the Egyptian War at Tel-el-Kebir.

Golf claimed him again on his return to this country and he became professional for a time at Winchester. But the English life did not suit Andra and he returned to St. Andrews and remained as a playing professional and caddie. He took part in numerous money matches between 1880 and 1900 and tied with the younger Willie Park in the Open of 1889, only to lose to him in the play-off. A notable victory he brought off was when he played a challenge match against J. H. Taylor for £50 and beat him. This was in 1895, just after 'J. H.' had become the first English professional to win the Open Championship. The victory was something of a salve to wounded Scottish pride.

After winning his match, 'Andra', who had been heavily backed by R. and A. members to win, was asked by a friend if they had remembered him in collecting their winnings.

"Aye," said Kirkaldy, with brusque satisfaction, "They've been mindfu', verra mindfu'."

In 1904 Andra succeeded Tom Morris as honorary professional to the R. and A., and although it could never be said that he mellowed, he became respected and regarded by the greatest in the land for his outspoken and undiplomatic comments, and also for his knowledge of the game.

His brother Hugh showed all the promise of becoming an outstanding golfer, but was another of a number of St. Andrews professionals of the era who were cut off young. These early deaths could often be traced to tuberculosis inherited from featherie-making ancestors. It was a notoriously unhealthy job.

Hugh Kirkaldy won the Open in 1891. He and Andra were only one example of golfing ability that ran in St. Andrews families. There were the Straths before them and of course, Old Tom Morris and Young Tom, and to a lesser extent his brother, J. O. F. Morris, a sound performer, but completely overshadowed by his peerless brother. There were Sandy Herd and his brother Fred. While Sandy was earning the distinction of becoming the first man to win the Open with the rubber-cored ball in 1902, Fred had won the American Open Championship four years earlier.

The Auchterlonie family contained five brothers who all played from scratch or better. Willie won the 1893 Open Championship, while Laurence took the American title in 1902, to equal the feat of the Herd brothers, Sandy and Fred, in winning international titles.

One of the finest amateur golfers St. Andrews produced in this era was Jamie Robb who won the Amateur Championship at Hoylake in 1906 after having been twice runner-up. Jamie reached the final four times. He represented Scotland for four years in international matches against England. After winning every local trophy around St. Andrews he took up a banking appointment in Prestwick and was a force in West of Scotland golfing circles for many years, before retiring to his native city.

Later still, the Ayton family of brothers distinguished themselves with their golf at home and in America. David, the eldest, was an even better teacher than player although he won a substantial amount of professional money. Laurie, also a fine teacher, won the Scottish professional championship and was high on the list in several Opens. Both sampled American golf successfully and helped expanding clubs there to prosperity. It was the youngest brother Alex who made his permanent home in the States and made a strong impact there for a time without actually winning any big championship. Their ancestors were founder members of the St. Andrews Golf Club, their great-grandfather and grandfather both being captains. Alex bequeathed a handsome legacy to the Club on his death.

Laurie Ayton, Jr., followed in the footsteps of his ancestors, one of the oldest golfing families in the country, in carving out a notable career for himself, with such success in professional events that he was selected a Ryder Cup player in 1949.

The family of the late Dr Kyle, St. Andrews were outstanding figures in amateur golf for many years from 1908 onwards. The elder son, E. P. Kyle, at the age of 19, reached the semi-final of the Open Amateur Championship; cleaned up, along with his brother Denis,

Every Living Open Champion in 1905

From left to right, standing; excluding first two:—J. H. Taylor, Jack White, Harold Hilton, John Ball, James Braid, Tom Morris (with stick), Bob Ferguson, Willie Auchterlonie, Jamie Anderson, D. Brown, Bob Martin, Willie Fernie

Sitting from left to right:—Sandy Herd, Harry Vardon, Willie Park, Jack Burns

Citizens exercise Rights of Recreation and of Bleaching Clothes on Old Course, 1875

all the chief local awards, and played for Scotland against England in 1925. On going to the Federated Malay States he won the championship there on five occasions.

Denis won the "Evening Telegraph" Cup—the equivalent of the Scottish Amateur Championship—in 1919; the Eden Tournament in 1920; represented Scotland in 1924 and 1930; and played for Great Britain in the 1924 Walker Cup match. Of the golfing sisters, Elsie was perhaps the most successful. She won the Scottish Ladies in 1909 and 1910 and in the 1908 she took Maud Titterton, the eventual winner, to the 24th hole in the sixth round. On retiring from medicine, she took up golf again and won the Dorset Ladies in 1953. Her sister Ida, who was runner-up in the 1911 Scottish Ladies, also represented Scotland twice. Audrey, the youngest of the sisters, played for Scotland three times and was runner-up in the 1922 Scottish Ladies. Richard, the youngest of the brothers, won the Duke of York Cup in 1920 but never attained international status.

Equally well-known were the Blackwell family, with Edward, Ernley, Jim and Walter all noted amateurs.

In amateur golf the Championship was resumed in 1920 after the First World War. It saw the emergence of Cyril Tolley, then an undergraduate at Oxford, and his fellow student, Roger Wethered, who became familiar figures at St. Andrews. In 1922 John Caven, who died in St. Andrews in 1982, lost at Prestwick to Sir Ernest Holderness. John Caven and Roger Wethered were members of the first official British Walker Cup Team which met the United States in 1922, and were the last survivors of that team. Wethered died early in March 1983, only a few months after Mr Caven. Holderness won again in 1924 at St. Andrews where he was favourite from the start. The championship did not return to the Old Course until Bobby Jones became the winner in historic 1930. Six years later, it was the dramatic turn of Hector Thomson to oust another invader, Jim Ferrier.

Walker Cup golf in 1924 introduced for the first time many noted American amateurs to the Old Course where the series in Britain were played for the first thirty years. The tremendous strides made by the Americans and their dedicated attitude to the game came as a revelation to their opponents and to St. Andrews galleries reared to the dilettante atmosphere of the R. and A. Players like Francis

Ouimet, Bob Gardner and Bob Jones set new standards of skill and efficiency for the swelling hordes of golfers in Britain and America. For their part, the friendly invaders found the Old Course, with its natural features and lay-out, an unknown and puzzling challenge.

St. Andrews was witnessing a new era in amateurism, as it was in professionalism — an era of 100 per cent concentration added to 100 per cent technical efficiency. The spark of genius in itself was not enough.

This background evoked intensified challenges by new home contestants — men like Jack McLean, Hector Thomson, A. T. Kyle, Ronnie White and Joe Carr. It brought as well fiercer thrills and patriotic dramas to the Old Course. Unavailing challenges they were, too, throughout the 'twenties and the 'thirties against the might and the fervour of the Americans.

Until 1938. Then the local galleries were to cheer to the echo the exploits of the British team in winning at last; cheer even more the sportsmanship and the high spirits of Charlie Yates and company in defeat, outside the venerable R. and A. Clubhouse.

Came the war and the Old Course saw a stream of new Americans as good as the old guard. Big Bill Campbell, Charles Coe, Billy Joe Patton, all conquered the course and their British opponents until 1971, when Britain claimed victory for a second time.

But John Caven, a respected resident in St. Andrews for many years, did not think that any of the subsequent American teams could compare with the inaugural team at the National Golf Links of America in 1922. John was a member of the first British team whose opposition included Bob Gardiner, Bobby Jones, Francis Ouimet, Jesse Guildford, and Jesse Sweetzer — all supreme golfers. "They were all champions," said John, himself one of the finest amateurs in Britain in his day.

One of the most gifted St. Andrews golfers of the earliest days of the present century was Fred Mackenzie who lacked only one asset in his formidable golf armoury . . . the urge to win. Essentially a golfer's player, he could play every shot in the book at will. As an amateur, he earned the unstinted praise of critical admirers. Bernard Darwin reckoned him one of the finest strikers of the ball he had ever seen, and the young Tommy Armour early tried to model himself on Mackenzie, who lacked only the champion's urge.

Another outstanding amateur was Ken Greig, winner of the Scottish Amateur title in 1930.

Several lads who received their early encouragement in the game at St. Andrews have made their mark in the higher echelons of golf. Perhaps the best known is George Will, who won the Scottish Boys and the British Youths Championships before turning professional in 1957. George became professional at Sundridge Park; represented Scotland in the World Cup three times, and won his place in the Ryder Cup three times.

Others include Alastair Low and Scott Macdonald, both British Universities Champions. Scott, son of St. Andrean Ian S. Macdonald, a former British Boy Champion, was a member of the victorious 1971 Walker Cup team and won the Boyd Quaich — the student international trophy — twice. Alastair prevented him from making it three in a row by taking the trophy in 1964. Others include Alex Soutar, former British Boy Champion, and Lachland Carver, Scottish Boy Champion of 1960.

MODERN ERA

To review the changes in golf in St. Andrews wrought by the modern era of big money tournaments and the glamour attached to the 'star' pros, a natural place to begin is with the last Open Championship before the war, that of 1939. Dick Burton, the winner, must count himself the unluckiest Open Champion of the century as war washed out all the usual perquisites he could expect to gain as holder of the title. He repelled the already familiar U.S. invasion, led by Johnny Bulla, with a final round of 71 that gave him victory by two strokes over the American. The latter was also second-equal in the first post-war Open of 1946, won by Snead, with a final round of 75 that was a tremendous score on a stormy day, when the Old Course was snarlingly showing its teeth.

Immediately after the war, the first big tournament with the Old Course as its venue was the "Daily Mail" in 1945. It was followed by Snead's Open in the following year. From then on the tournament circuits of the world have become increasingly rich fields. The professional set-up bears no relation to the early days.

The Old was kept busy with other major golf events as the game rocketed in popularity all over the world. In the 39 years between 1945 and 1984, a total of 36 major national and international events has been held in St. Andrews. These include eight Open Championships (1946, 1955, 1957, 1960, 1964, 1970, 1978 and 1984); four Walker Cup matches (1947, 1955, 1971 and 1975); five Amateur Championships (1950, 1958, 1963, 1976 and 1981); two British Ladies Championships (1965 and 1975); five Scottish Amateur Championships (1951, 1959, 1965, 1971 and 1976); three Scottish Ladies Championships (1950, 1961 and 1973); Daily Mail (1945); Dunlop Masters (1949); Spalding (1947 and 1948); Martini (1962); PGA Match Play (1954 and 1979); Alcan Golfer of the Year and Alcan International Championship (1967); Sunbeam Electric Scottish Open Championship (1973); St. Andrews Trophy — Great Britain v. Rest of Europe (1976 and 1982); Youth International (Scotland v. England) (1982); European Amateur Team Championship (1981); and British Youths Championship (1982).

In addition, St. Andrews was signally honoured in being chosen to hold the inaugural Commonwealth Tournament in 1954; the Ladies' Commonwealth Tournament in 1959; the inaugural Eisenhower World Peace Trophy in 1958; and the Jubilee Walker Cup of 1971, as well as the succeeding event of 1975.

The 1946 Open Championship on the Old Course marked the first introduction of full crowd control in Britain — a vital and mounting problem in big-time golf to that date. Col. M. E. Lindsay of the R. and A. was the pioneer who organised the spade work. The arrangements worked excellently when 12,000 spectators thronged the course on the final day. The Walker Cup of 1947 was a period of unseasonably cold weather on the Old, but the Americans withstood it well, to win by 8-4.

Around this time, prominent St. Andrews amateurs the late Andrew Dowie and the late J. L. Lindsay had been in the eye of the Walker Cup selectors, although neither was chosen. Dowie had a great record in Scottish tournaments and for a time held the amateur record for the Old with a 71.

A huge entry for the 1950 Amateur was swelled by a formidable American list. Frank Stranahan won the title for the second time, but a happy memory was an astonishing performance by Cyril Tolley in reaching the semi at the age of 53. This event brought the question of slow play very much to a head. Stranahan, a central figure in the criticism, still left St. Andrews an emphatically popular player with old and young, despite an unpromising and somewhat truculent start to his public relations. He beat Dick Chapman in the final by superlative golf. Chapman returned many times afterwards to St. Andrews.

The most historic year in golf legislation for two centuries — since 1754 — was 1951 when the R. and A., the Dominions' representatives and those of the United States Golf Association met at St. Andrews in a four-day conference and made a number of important decisions to unify golf rules throughout the world. Among them was the tardy abolition of the stymie and the equally tardy approval by the R. and A. of the centre-shaft putter which had been banned in Britain for nearly half-a-century.

Appropriately, it was in this year that Francis Ouimet, once a caddie, became the first American ever to be selected Captain of the

R. and A. — a highly popular, as well as a significantly diplomatic choice. His portrait has an honoured place in the clubhouse.

A confessed lover of the Old Course, Peter Thomson, the young Australian, emerged at the "News of the World" match-play championship of 1954 on the Old Course. He reached the final to defeat J. Fallon, Huddersfield, after two extra holes. Thomson's fighting qualities were never better demonstrated than in that "News of the World". He showed then that his smiling, amiable countenance masked the grim determination and concentration of the champion. In the fourth round he stood two down and two holes to play against Scotland's John Panton. Thomson eagled the Road Hole and followed with a birdie three at the last and then he went on to win the match at the 22nd with a huge putt. In the next round he had a homeric match against Bobby Locke who led him most of the way until the last hole. Then, in the final, over 36 holes, he was quickly four down to sparkling golf by Johnny Fallon. Not until the 34th hole did he square the game by holing an enormous putt. The only time he was ahead in the match was when he won the championship at the 38th hole.

In the following year, Thomson won the Open on the Old Course — his second of five Open titles — after being hard-pressed all the way by the self-same Johnny Fallon, and Frank Jowle. American competitors were Ed Furgol, who had won the States title, and the great Byron Nelson. Furgol disliked the Old after successive 7s at the long 14th. Nelson found it a first class test of championship golf, but "could not read the greens". He added: "Your crowd control is magnificent. You will not be surprised to learn that we Americans have copied the St. Andrews system."

Peter Thomson from the first was a St. Andrews enthusiast, and his record on the Old Course gives full reason for his love of it. "I am the best plugger of the Old Course" he said after his 1955 win. "It is the best course in the world and there is none like it. I am more convinced of that the more I play it" — words very similar to those of Bobby Jones twenty years before — and repeated often years later.

Joe Conrad, the American Walker Cup player, who finished first amateur, subscribed to the same view. He thought the Old was the finest course he had played on.

The qualifying rounds for 1955, one on the New Course, gave rise to one of the happiest newspaper headings for long enough. The record of 63 (30-33) for the course, believed by many to be more difficult than the Old, was set by Frank Jowle, and should stand for years. It was delightfully written up as "Cheek by Jowle!"

The Walker Cup, played in May of the same year, was also succinctly described in newsprint as: "Dismal Result in Dismal Weather". Britain were thrashed 10-2. David Blair, one of the two home single winners, had to shoot a 69—the best figures of the series, to beat Conrad on the last green.

The year 1955 at St. Andrews also stood out historically. It was the first occasion in Britain that two outstanding golfing events, the Walker Cup in May, and the Open Championship in July, were played on the same course in one year. It was also the first year in Britain that the televising of two big golf events was introduced. The now-familiar television towers first erected on the Old Course, and for which permanent wiring was laid, that year cast their first elongated shadows along the borders of the Links.

This film recording of golf events by television camera very quickly took on a unique significance in golf history.

Two years later, in 1957, the Open was again being held on the Old Course. Bobby Locke, that great South African, now a veteran competitor, was on the last green, his ball two feet from the flag, and with three shots for the coveted title. The TV cameras were turning when he lifted his ball and marked it to allow his opponent, 'Aussie' Bruce Crampton, to hole out. Then Locke duly played the stroke that won him the title.

Some days later the champion stood in fear of disqualification! The story had gone out that he had failed to replace his ball at his mark on the green, and he had holed out from another position. He was therefore liable to disqualification under the rules.

Just after the championship Locke had said: "This is the greatest day of my life—to win the Open Championship on the Old Course of St. Andrews."

Was the cup of triumph going to be dashed from his very lips?

Eight days afterwards, he was invited to see the television record of the last stages of the Open. It showed that when he marked his ball on the last green he had not replaced it in the original position from which he had lifted it. He had broken the rules of golf!

Locke immediately telephoned the R. and A. and settled down to wait for an official ruling that would decide the issue once and for all. He received the following happy reply:

"The Championship Committee intend to take no action with regard to the incident on the last green which appeared in the television film of the Open. Your winning score remains at 279. A penalty may, in exceptional circumstances, be waived if the Committee consider the action warranted. This Committee considers that when a competitor has three for the Open Championship from two feet, and then commits a technical error which brings him no possible advantage, exceptional circumstances then exist, and the decision should be given accordingly, in equity and in the spirit of the game. Please feel free to show this letter to anyone.—N. C. Selway, Chairman, Championship Committee."

The strain and stress of tournament golf is probably the greatest ordeal in sport. To give a picture of the strain under which Locke had stood on that last green—an ordeal that is borne by all champions to be—let us recall an interview with him just afterwards.

"I needed a five at the last hole to win the title. After my drive I laid a No. 8 iron 'dead' for a birdie three. A colossal yell rose from the crowd of 10,000 around that green that made me shake from head to foot. I took my caddie by the arm and gave him a squeeze, so tightly; otherwise I felt I would burst.

"As I walked that 130 yards to the green the cheers were deafening. I could not believe my fortune! There was another tremendous roar as my putt dropped. I took off my cap and put my head hard back to prevent the tears that were so very close. After 21 years the Old Course had opened up its heart to a competitor who has always had the utmost respect for its unique difficulties."

The agonising nerve ordeal of the final stages was even more shatteringly demonstrated in 1933. One of the toughest American competitors, Leo Diegel, stood with victory in his grasp after a great approach to the last green. He missed the putt, but still had a two-footer to tie. Such was the pressure on him that Diegel petrified himself and completely failed even to hit the ball!

Joyce Wethered, despite apparent calm throughout her terrific match with Glenna Collett, fainted immediately she reached the clubhouse. Bobby Jones was violently sick after his 1930 triumph.

It has always been tough at the top!

No year stands out more memorably in the hallowed history of golf in St. Andrews than 1958. It witnessed three great golfing events; nostalgic presentation of the freedom of the city to Bobby Jones; the inaugural tournament, for which the Old Course had the honour of being chosen, of the Eisenhower World Team Trophy, and the Amateur Championship for that year. Bobby Jones, as non-playing captain of the American team, was given an unforgettable reception by the town.

The thousands of spectators at this great inaugural team tournament, saw a terrific climax in the last hour of the event, in which Britain and America both lost chances of winning the trophy outright. Then in a tense and thrilling replay between America and Australia, the fine golfers from "down under" won by two strokes. The shades of Old Davie Robertson and Peter Anderson, the two St. Andrews pioneers and the grandfather and father of golf in Australia, must have smiled broadly!

Earlier in the year, the Amateur Championship resulted in a popular and merited win for the lanky Irishman, Joe Carr, over England's Alan Thirlwell, by 3 and 2.

A decision was made to close the Old Course in the winter of 1959 for four months to nurse it for the coming Open Chaampionship. Two big events had taken their toll in a summer of drought and heat. The Ladies' Commonwealth Tournament, played in June '59, by teams from Australia, Canada, New Zealand, South Africa and Britain, was refreshing and a revelation to spectators for the grace, skill, sportsmanship — and speed of the top ladies of the world in action. Then in July the Scottish Amateur attracted a record entry and was handsomely won by Dr Frank Deighton who beat R. M. K. Murray by 6 and 5.

The Centenary Open in 1960 was eminently memorable for its record crowds, record scores and notable incidents. These included the most violent cloudburst in St. Andrews for exactly fifty years. The R. and A. steps leading down to the course were converted within minutes into a waterfall. By an amazing coincidence, it was during the Jubilee Open half-a-century earlier, in 1910, that a cloudburst on the Old Course washed out a day's play. Then James Braid was told on the 16th tee that scores were void but stoically and cannily he finished his round for a tremendous 77. It was only justice that he was the eventual Jubilee winner, after possibly the greatest round of his career.

The 1960 centenary champion was Kel Nagle, the 'quiet Australian' who successfully withstood Arnold Palmer breathing down his neck all the way in on his final round of 71 for 278. He was just one ahead of the great American, with Gary Player, the equally magnetic South African, trailing.

Both professional and amateur records were smashed. Peter Allis—"Allis in Wonderland"—had a wonder 66, while Joe Carr, the mercurial Irish amateur, shot a 68. Then Bernard Hunt equalled Allis's record and Guy Wolstenholme compiled the best amateur aggregate so far for the Old of 283.

No more brilliant list of the world's 'greats' was ever told to 'Play away, please' than by Jimmy Alexander. During the 39 years he occupied the starting box of the Old Course, Jimmy of the stentorian voice was the world's best-known starter, until his death shortly after the Centenary Open. A veteran of the First World War, he was one of the best one-armed golfers in Britain. His autograph books contained the signatures of the world's most famous golfers and of the many celebrities in other fields who came to St. Andrews, including that of the Duke of Windsor as Prince of Wales, and of President Eisenhower.

The television era in British golf was launched on the Old Course in the Centenary Open year when two matches were played for television viewing programmes. First, in July, Arnold Palmer and Gary Player were antagonists in a big money match reminiscent of a century before—but with a modern twist. Every stroke was to be seen by millions of television viewers all over the world! Palmer was winner by five shots and he reserved most of the excitement for the last three holes at which stage the little South African had brought back a half-way deficit of five shots down to two. But Palmer shot an inward 34 finishing 3, 3, 3, for a round of 70. Later in the year, Henry Cotton played his veteran American contemporary, Gene Sarazen, in the inaugural match of a television series designed to show viewers the best-known courses of the world.

The first colour television film of a golf match in Britain concluded in St. Andrews in July, 1966. Jack Nicklaus, winner of the Open at Muirfield a week before, Arnold Palmer and Gary Player, the globe-trotting musketeers of modern golf, played a series of three games on the Scottish courses of Gleneagles and Carnoustie. It finished on the Old Course where they were watched by a crowd of several thousands. Their respective scores on the Old were 70, 71 and 72, and the result of the match overall was a tie on 218 strokes each. Again, it was the most modern version of the old-time challenge matches that a century before were played between golfers from as far afield as Musselburgh, Montrose and even Prestwick! The three golfers in this case were back in America within a few hours of leaving the Old Course!

Peter Thomson again showed his mastery of the wiles of the Old Course when the Martini tournament was played in 1962. He won it with the brilliant aggregate of 275. This included a 66, the highlight of which was an eagle three at the long 5th hole.

Local honour, harder to win in these days of intensified competition, came in 1963 when St. Andrews schoolboy Alec Soutar won the British Boy's Championship against the odds — the first St. Andrean to do it since 1932 when Ian Macdonald was the holder. In the Amateur on the Old that year, Michael Lunt defeated 48-year-old J. G. Blackwell, captain-to-be of the R. and A. and bearer of a name noted in St. Andrews and in the Club's records.

From overseas, the challenge for the 1964 Open on the Old Course was star-studded. Tragic Tony Lema, the ultimate winner, was accompanied by Jack Nicklaus, Gary Player, Peter Thomson, Bob Charles, the left-hander, a Chinaman, L. H. Lu from Hong Kong and a host of other nationalities.

One should rightly say that Lema was preceded by the other overseas players. He arrived on the eve of the event, in time for only two practice rounds and then had the temerity to beat the field and the Old Course. But Lema had the foresight to engage the experienced "Young Tip" Anderson as his caddie, and "Tip" provided the local knowledge that abetted a superlative display of grace, power and putting artistry by the American. He spreadeagled the field with 73, 68, 68 and then wound up with a great 70. He was under pressure then from the powerful Nicklaus who reduced the extended Old Course to very ordinary measurements with consistent length that was unmatched. But Nicklaus "Just couldn't get the putting going". His systematic survey of the course in practice was a revelation of painstaking groundwork and preparation to many of our own home professionals, but it was the champagne of Lema's sparkling golf that left the most memorable impression of a clear five shot win. His tragic death in 1966 was deeply deplored in St. Andrews.

The British Ladies' Open Championship in 1965 gave St. Andrews and Scottish enthusiasts generally an opportunity of seeing the strong challenge that France presented at that time. Their winning player, Brigit Varangot, was the most accomplished short-game golfer in the field, and won on that asset. To match Mrs Belle Robertson, the Scots finalist, England had in the field a whole host of promising young girls, such as Susan Armitage, Pam Tredinnick, Mrs Bonallack, her sister, Shirley Ward, and others who responded inspiringly to the challenge of the Old Course. The French contingent also included Miss Lacoste, who fulfilled her promise by winning the American Women's Open Championship in 1967. The first overseas challenger to do so, she was also its youngest winner.

A new era of tournament golf opened in St. Andrews when the Alcan Champion Golfer of the Year event was inaugurated on the Old Course in October, 1967. It was notable for two records which it created. One was local; the other international.

The international record was that the first prize, won by American Gay Brewer after a play-off with his compatriot, Billy Casper, was the world's biggest offered to that date, a sum of £19,675. This could have been £21,462 if the special bonus award of £1,787 for the week's best aggregate had not been annexed by Peter Thomson, Australia, winner of the subsidiary International tourney run in conjunction with the Golfer of the Year Championship. Thomson's winnings were £4,250 for his aggregate of 281; Brewer, two strokes worse, won £15,000 more!

More historically impressive was the second record. The Alcan was the first golf event for which permission was ever given to allow the Old Course to be brought into use on a Sunday.

The world Press hailed the 1970 championship as the greatest and most thrill-packed Open witnessed within living memory. Its five days were crammed with dramatic incident. Fittingly, the winner it produced was the most powerful and probably the finest golfer of modern times, Jack Nicklaus of the U.S.

But only after a 283-aggregate tie with fellow American Doug Sanders who wilted in the nerve-racking tension of the final green with a tragic three-putt.

It was truly a record-breaking Open. The world's top players competed; 81,000 spectators were attracted, the biggest golf-watching crowds anywhere; those galleries saw the Old Course record shattered and they watched the Old Course exact full revenge.

All the excitement and drama of a titanic week was distilled into the eighteen-hole Sunday play-off, the first-ever in St. Andrews. In a gruelling match, underdog Sanders tenaciously pulled back from four strokes behind at the 14th to a single shot down with the last hole to play. The galleries had been spellbound by superb play from both men in tricky conditions.

With the final tee came the moment of imperishable memory. Facing downwind, Nicklaus paused, considered. He peeled off a sweater, and the crowd sighed in anticipation of the big hit. The Big Bear shaped up, swung and unleashed a colossal drive. None of the 7,000 Sunday watchers had seen before, or were ever likely to see again, a ball hit so far, with such controlled fury. It carried almost to Sanders' long drive, galloped up the Valley of Sin and over the Home Hole Green. On and on, and up into the grassy bank beyond, to nestle in the long grass under the very noses of the craning spectators jamming the barrier fence.

The lie was treacherous, but the niblick recovery shot was perfection. Down went the putt for a birdie three and victory. For once the poker-faced Nicklaus gave rein to his emotions; his sky-hurled putter just missed the disconsolate Sanders' head on its descent. The crowds surged in to pay their tribute.

In a brief five days the Old had produced a full gamut of emotions and of weather. Neil Coles, in perfect conditions, broke the record with a glorious 65, the while Tony Jacklin, the holder and U.S. Champion, was stringing together the finest nine consecutive holes yet compiled on the Old, thus: 3, 3, 3, 4, 4, 4, 3, 3, 2 – 29. He stood eight under par at the 14th when the heavens opened just after he had hit a magnificent drive. Sheets of water blinded him as he shaped up to his second, and Jacklin cut the ball into an unplayable lie. By then the greens were flooded. He completed his round in the early dawn of the next morning, but the magic was gone – 6, 4, 5, 5, 4 for 67. A wonderful score, it was but a pale shadow of what might have been.

St. Andrews tradition was upheld by John Richardson, a local man who went south as a club professional and blossomed as a tournament golfer to finish the second best Scot with a £750 cheque.

The Walker Cup of 1971 was a match of triumph for British golf. For only the second time in the history of the event, the home side won and so made the jubilee match memorable. Victory for St. Andrews was all the sweeter as both home successes have been scored on the Old. The scenes in 1971 afterwards were almost as jubilant as those of the first win 33 years earlier.

A few months later the Old Course saw the youngest ever winner of the Scottish Amateur Championship emerge as champion when Sandy Stephen, Lundin Links, beat veteran Charlie Green, one of the Walker Cup winning team. A terrific thunderstorm reminiscent of the one which a year earlier had brought Tony Jacklin's scintillating round in the Open to a summary end, halted this match too. Stephen was two up at the fifteenth and only one more hole was necessary on the Sunday to give him the title.

In 1971 Bing Crosby visited St. Andrews, and with a little encouragement from his friend, J. K. Wilson, offered to endow a trophy to be contested between the senior golfers who are members of golf clubs in St. Andrews. The inaugural tournament in 1972 was won by St. Andrews clubmaker John Robertson. The Bing Crosby Tournament is held each year in September so that R. and A. members attending the Autumn meeting may have the opportunity to take part.

There was another visitor to St. Andrews in 1972. Mr Zenya Hamada, a Japanese business tycoon, poet, actor and dramatist, unfolded his plans for constructing a replica of the Old Course on some 300 acres of land which he had purchased near Tokyo. The Town Council had no objection, so Mr Hamada made another announcement – he would set up a Trust for the benefit of St. Andrews and of golf, and he backed this up immediately with a cheque for £50,000 and a promise of more.

In the following year Mr Hamada asked for some whin seeds from the Old Course bushes so that he could plant them in his new course. He offered, in return, to send 1,000 cherry trees to be planted in the town. Some Town Councillors objected but eventually the Town Council relented and the exchange was made. One month later Mr Hamada made another gift of £50,000, bringing the total capital value of the Trust to £100,000. An independent Trust was set up and it makes grants and interest-free loans to a wide range of voluntary bodies in the town.

Strangely, the Scottish Professional title has been played for only once on the Old Course. This was in 1973 and once again the Course's ability to produce super-charged dramatic spectacle was proven. A record crowd for the event saw Australian Graham Marsh run away with the title with the most amazing finish ever witnessed on the Old. He played the last five holes in an incredible five under par to win by five strokes. His 4, 3, 4, 3, 2 included an eagle at the last where he drove the green and sank a fifteen foot putt.

The Scottish Ladies' also was held over the Old Course in 1973 when Mrs Janette Wright, winner 12 years earlier on the same circuit, beat off her younger challengers for her fourth title in five finals.

HIGH DRAMA

COUNTLESS sporting dramas arising from the personal combat of championships and golf's obsessive grip have been enacted on the courses of the world. The huge galleries generate their own intensely pent-up atmosphere by their excitement and their spontaneous applause, but even more by their pregnant silences. St. Andrews' venerable Old Course where so many events of world importance have been fought out, has been the stage of innumerable such memorable scenes. Because of its historic background and atmosphere, these often have taken on a deeper, epic quality that has etched them indelibly on the memory of participants and witnesses alike.

Yet the greatest of golf occasions, and certainly the most emotionally charged, while it concerned St. Andrews intimately, took place not on the Old Course at all. It happened in the Younger Graduation Hall of the University of St. Andrews. The 'gallery' was a select audience of the finest amateur golfers of thirty nations; the top golf writers of the world, and the golf-imbued people of St. Andrews . . . those of them lucky enough to squeeze into the hall.

The date was 1958 and the occasion was unique in the annals of golf. The first Eisenhower Trophy was to be played on the Old Course by the representatives of the thirty assembled nations.

As the highest tribute they could pay, in token of their deepest admiration and abiding affection for the world's greatest golfer of this day, the people of St. Andrews were about to present to Mr Robert Tyre Jones of Atlanta, U.S.A., the freedom of the city. Few men previously had been so honoured in its long history as Bobby Jones, and only one other was an American. He was Benjamin Franklin, the great Philadelphia scientist, and the date was October, 1759.

Now, in 1958, in the packed hall the audience cheered the crippled athlete to the echo as he rose from his chair behind the wide platform that has seated some of the world's most distinguished figures in every walk of life. Not one had evoked more heart-warming affection than pervaded the hall throughout that memorable evening. It swelled and intensified through their guest's simple speech of nostalgic reminiscence. Release came at the end in a catharsis of applause of shattering spontaneity. The new Freeman had to fight hard to check unbidden tears; tears of emotion and affection glistened in the eyes of hard-bitten journalists and unemotional, dour Scotsmen.

As he later confessed, it was the proudest occasion in the life of the man described as the most distinguished golfer of all time.

The writer was fortunate to be present and to record every word uttered by Bobby Jones in his address. Presiding over the gathering was Provost Robert Leonard of St. Andrews, who outlined the reasons for the ceremony.

"We feel drawn to Mr Jones," he said, "by ties of affection and personal regard of a particularly cordial nature, and we know that he himself has declared his own enduring affection for this place and for its people.

"Like many cordial and enduring partnerships it was not, I think, a case of love at first sight. Few St. Andreans paid attention to the young American golfer who came for the British Open of 1921. I believe that, for his part, the first impression that he formed of the Old Course was something less than favourable. And there—with any other person and any other place—the matter might well have rested. But back he came in 1930 to master the intricacies of golf at St. Andrews, as they have never been mastered before, even by our giants of the 19th century, and to win his way, not only to the Open Championship, but into the hearts of St. Andrews people from that day to this."

The Provost recalled the description of that moment when Jones became champion, by Bernard Darwin, most polished of British golf writers.

"Many vivid pictures remain in my mind's eye from this day, but there is one in particular. Bobby lay just short of the Home Green, in the hollow called the Valley of Sin. He ran his long putt up dead, and the crowd stormed up the slope and waited breathless on the crest for a moment. He popped his ball in, and the next instant there was to be seen no green and no Bobby – nothing but a black and seething mass from which there ultimately emerged the victor on enthusiastic shoulders, and bearing aloft his famous putter, 'Calamity Jane' over his head in a frantic effort to preserve it! Nothing could ever surpass the achievement of his memorable year of 1930 when he won all four major championships."

Mr Jones told Provost Leonard he appreciated the fact of his first encounter with the Old Course being recalled. When he gave up at the 11th it was Hill Bunker he got into, not Strath. And he did not hit his ball into the Eden when he got out, because he never did get out of Hill Bunker! He returned in 1929 with the Walker Cup team, and in the interval, he had done a lot of thinking and a lot of practice. He set about studying the course and pretty soon found out that local knowledge was a really important thing.

"To play that course you have to study it, and the more you study it the more you learn. The more you learn the more you study it. I have to say this that after my chastisement she must have been satisfied and never let me lose another contest. When I say that, the reason why I won was largely due to what she did to the other fellow." (Ltr.)

"But the memories of St. Andrews that really mean most to me – I am afraid to talk about them because I get a little too emotional – are not entirely to do with championships. After all, if you enter a tournament, and don't cheat and happen to make the lowest score, they have to give you a cup.

"But you people of St. Andrews have a sensitivity and an ability to extend cordiality in an ingenious way.

"When I won the Amateur in 1930 and got back home, I received through the post, a perfect miniature of the Amateur Championship Trophy. It was an exquisite thing, perfect in every detail, down to the names inscribed on it; there was an inscription on it, which, at this moment I could not trust myself to repeat. That miniature came to me with the simple message that it was from my fellow-members of the R. and A. It has remained my prized possession."

Mr Jones then went on to refer to his 1936 visit and his wonderful welcome then from the people of St. Andrews. He added:

"I could take out of my life everything except my experiences at St. Andrews and I would still have had a rich and full life."

At the end of the prolonged and tremendous applause, he added:

"There are two very important words in the English language that are much mis-used and abused. They are 'friend' and 'friendship'." Later in his address he added: "When I say, with due regard for the meaning of the word, that I am your friend, I have pledged to you the ultimate in loyalty and devotion. In some respects friendship may even transcend love, for in true friendship there is no place for jealousy. When without more, I say that you are my friends, it is possible that I may be imposing upon you a greater burden than you are willing to assume. But when you have made me aware on many occasions that you have a kindly feeling towards me, and when you have honoured me at every means within your command, then when I call you my friend, I am at once affirming my high regard and affection for you and declaring my complete faith in you and trust in the sincerity of your expressions. And so, my fellow citizens of St. Andrews, it is with this appreciation of the full sense of the word that I salute you as my friends."

"I hope I have not been too sentimental on this theme of friendship, but it is one that is so important at this time. It is another element of the sensitivity that you people have — a wonderful warm relationship. . . . I just want to say that this is the finest thing that has ever happened to me. Whereas that little cup was first in my heart, now this occasion at St. Andrews will take first place always. I like to think about it in this way that, now officially I have the right to feel at home in St. Andrews as in fact, I always have done."

The hall rose solidly and spontaneously to the speaker with applause that lasted for several minutes. An unforgettable occasion for everyone there! A gathering of a more solemn kind assembled in the old Town Church of St. Andrews — the church of which old Tom Morris had been an elder — in May, 1972 to pay tribute to their golfing freeman some months after his death. Men and women from all walks of life in the old city mingled with members of the Royal and Ancient Club from many parts of the world. They sat, sombre and remote in their individual memories, behind the widow and family of the man they knew as Bobby Jones. The simple Scottish memorial service was conducted by the chaplain of the R. and A. and a moving tribute was paid by his greatest British rival, Roger Wethered.

The memory of Bobby Jones was perpetuated on the Old Course by giving his name to the Tenth Hole. Later, a Trust Fund was set up by his friends in this country and in United States to provide exchange scholarships for students of St. Andrews University and Emory College, where Bobby Jones took his degree in law.

In the realms of high drama on the golf links shots of magical execution that are conjured up when they are most needed rarely happen. When they do, these 'miracle' shots invariably mark the special quality of the champion.

For that reason, and because it was possibly the first recorded epic shot, a pitch by Allan Robertson at the Road Hole must be recalled, from the dim past of more than a century ago. Robert Chambers tells us that Allan was partnering Mr Erskine of the R. and A. in a foursome for a very big money wager against Willie Park, the Musselburgh pro, and Mr Hastie, also of the Club. At the end of the third and last round Park and partner were one up with two holes to go.

Mr Campbell of Saddell, another R. and A. member, was a spectator. Never averse to a gamble, he offered £15 to £5 on Park. Allan's side seemed doomed when Park pitched well on the green. Mr Erskine, 'playing the odd', put Allan on the road. Playing 'the two more' as it was termed, the champion produced his devastating blow. With the utmost care and precision, he pitched his ball onto the narrow top footpath bounding the green to within a fraction of his mark. Slowly the ball began to trickle and run on to the green. On and on it went, until it stopped — in the hole!

Stunned, Mr Hastie went for the hole and sent his putt a full 4½ feet past. Park, for once, was unforgivably 'never up' and they lost the hole. What was worse Willie Park, thoroughly rattled, topped his drive from the last tee into the Swilcan, to lose the match, the hole and the money.

Many, many great shots have been witnessed since at the famous Road Hole green, but few have had this 'miracle' champion quality.

In the Centenary Open Championship of 1960, memorable for many incidents, none was more thrilling than the grandstand finish provided by the winner, Kel Nagle, and Arnold Palmer, runner-up. The climax again came at the Road Hole, the notorious 17th. Nagle had played it well and had to sink an awkward 8 foot putt for a 4. He was shaping up for the putt when ahead, on the 18th green, a tremendous shout rent the air. It told him the Palmer had sunk a birdie for a 68!

This meant Nagle simply had to sink his putt, and, bravely, he did! He needed a par 4 at the last to win the title, and the Australian produced a wonder pitch to within three feet of the flag. It was a shot beyond praise under such pressure and with milling thousands pressing on him. Poor Vicenzo, his partner, was swamped by the crowd. Little wonder that he pitched short and then proceeded to 3-putt for a 6, costing himself £170 in the process! He was destined to sustain a disaster of much greater magnitude some years later when a simple formality oversight cost him the American Masters title.

Nagle failed to hole his downhill putt for the birdie but just had a tap-in to become the Centenary Champion. He did so before a record crowd for any British golf event, of 30,000 spectators.

Exactly one hundred years earlier, in 1860, a champion's determination was displayed on a more sustained and heroic scale. Captain, later Admiral Maitland Dougal of Scotscraig, performed it in winning the R. and A. Autumn Meeting.

One of the best players in the Club, Maitland Dougal was preparing to set out to play in the Medal, with a raging October gale at its worst. The rain was lashing down. The news came that a vessel was in distress in the bay. Preparations were made to man the lifeboat which was housed within two hundred yards of the first tee. Volunteers were slow to come forward. Some of the fishermen felt it was courting death to no purpose. R. and A. members offered them money to crew the boat, and Captain Maitland Dougal left the first tee and took over the stroke oar himself, as the best example of encouragement to the fishermen.

For five hours the lifeboat was at sea, with the Admiral straining at his key oar. The vessel they hoped to save was one of five big fishing boats that had got into trouble in the bay and were drifting helplessly towards the rocks. The crew had thrown over their trawl to act as a drag, without avail, and were fearfully and helplessly awaiting death. A steamship also came to the rescue and, by superb seamanship, protected the most vulnerable fishing vessel enough from the seas to allow the lifeboat to get alongside and take its crew off in tremendous seas before the yawl was smashed on the rocks.

After five hours at the oars, Maitland Dougal hurriedly got into dry clothes and went straight on to the first tee. To counteract the terrific gale still raging, he bored a hole in his gutta ball, and put in some buckshot to weight the ball, and so keep it low in the wind. In the upshot, he completed his round and returned the winning score of 112, to win the coveted Medal . . . a Corinthian heroic *par excellence*.

The fishermen who manned the boat were well rewarded afterwards, as the members had promised.

Curiously, the Admiral was associated with another fierce gale. From his home overlooking the River Tay, he was the only person to witness the blowing down of the first Tay Bridge in 1879 and see a whole train plunge into the river with the loss of everyone aboard.

Another single shot of the 'miracle' variety from the bag of a champion is worth recording for the way in which it illustrates the essential quality of the man who played it. Old Tom Morris was the player. He was in the bents (thick, coarse grass) at the High Hole, after having played the 'two more'. Captain Broughton, his opponent, jeeringly said: "You'd best give up the hole, Tom!"

"No, I micht hole this," calmly replied Tom.

"I'll give you £50 if you do," promptly replied the Captain.

"Done," said Tom, and he holed a seemingly impossible shot from the rough!

The next morning Captain Broughton arrived with fifty golden sovereigns for Tom. "Take it away," said Tom. "I would not have it. We were in fun."

Later, asked if the story were true, Tom laughed. "You should have seen the Captain's face when the ball dropped in that hole!"

Only once has St. Andrews lost its dignity and its natural assumption that golf is all. The man who brought about this unprecedented lapse from tradition was himself a confessed 'golf-maniac'. Yet when the whole town poured down to the first tee to watch him play in the 1950 Amateur Championship, it was not his golf that was the attraction, but the man himself, Bing Crosby, they had gone to see.

There were some of the Championship organisers who were not too happy about his entry. Was it a piece of show-biz publicity? Or was he entering *bona fide*, as a golfer?

Bing responded magnificently, and showed them that he was. In the only round he played he revealed a flash of that special magnetic gift of rising to the occasion. A cold wind was tearing in from the sea, but over 7,000 spectators, many of them from beyond the town, but still a goodly proportion of St. Andreans and R. and A. members, known for their single-mindedness for golf, were there.

The American film star, then the consummate glamour personality to most of the world, was paired against local golfer, J. K. Wilson of the St. Andrews Club. Bing started off with a great winning birdie at the first, halved the second in par and then won the third with another great birdie. The gallery was entranced. Crosby ultimately lost 3 and 2 to Wilson, but he had demonstrated to his thousands of fans that he was, indeed, a golfer worthy of playing in the championship.

In such circumstances, St. Andrews excused itself for its lapse from dignity and its affront to the royal and ancient game in placing a mere film star even temporarily in higher esteem than a golfer. Incidentally, his opponent still bears in the town and always will, the nickname, 'Bing' Wilson! The film star subsequently donated a trophy to be played for by senior golfers of the town and R. and A. He came to St. Andrews specially to take in the inaugural event.

Most tragic of unforgettable golfing occasions was the twilight of a champion. At the height of his fame, the unbeaten Young Tom Morris had gone to North Berwick to meet a challenge from the Park brothers partnered by his father.

In the midst of the game, a telegram messenger pushed his way through to Old Tom, his father, who read the wire with stunned incredulity. The match was stopped and Tom told his son that his young wife was seriously ill and they must make all speed for St. Andrews. A second telegram came before they left, with the news that mother and child were both dead. Tom kept the news from his distraught son.

One of the gentlemen 'backers' placed his yacht at their disposal to take the pair across the Forth to St. Andrews as speedily as possible. A silent, melancholy group made its way over the calm waters on that September day of 1875, and only when he espied the party of friends waiting anxiously at the pier, did Tom break the news as gently as he could to his heart-broken son, that his wife of little more than a year and her unborn child were lost.

A mournful procession made its way along the Scores and past the grim walls of St. Andrews Castle to the home of Tom Morris at the Links. Compassionately, all eyes were averted from the tragic figure of the young champion as he stared unseeingly and uncomprehendingly ahead. At the house, the parish minister, the Rev. Dr Boyd, was waiting: "I was in the house whenever they arrived. What can one say at such an hour? I never forgot the poor young man's stricken look, and how, all of a sudden, he started up and cried, 'It's not true!'"

Young Tom, the peerless, invincible champion, played two more games of golf, both to honour previous arrangements. Three months later, on Christmas morning, he passed away in bed. It was said he really died at that moment that his father, with the little harbour of St. Andrews slowly nearing, gently broke the news to him of his loss. The tragic truth, behind the screen of Victorian euphemism is that Young Tom, in a brief and unaccustomed excess of drink, succeeded only too well in drowning his sorrow.

The characteristics that set the champion apart are as clearly evident in the realm of feminine sport as in the male. Lady Heathcote-Amory, as Joyce Wethered, was a magnificent but reluctant champion. She is still reckoned the finest-ever woman player. She possessed the essential champion quality and it made her an invincible champion in women's golf, almost against her will.

On the Old Course in particular, but always where she played, Miss Wethered revealed a completely new brand of women's golf, of which impeccable, relentless accuracy of every shot was the feature. Her length from the tee was not far short of the top amateur men; unlike them, she always finished in the middle of the fairway; her seconds seldom missed the green; she three-putted less than any women and most men. Her whole game was devastatingly devoid of error, stemming from a beautiful action, and motivated by the champion's quality of single-minded concentration. She loved and respected the Old Course and regarded her Ladies' Championship there as the highlight of her title wins.

Classic example of that special quality which set her apart came at the 16th green of the Old Course in her epic Ladies' Championship final of 1929 against Glenna Collett, the outstanding American champion. A vital putt faced Miss Wethered to win the hole. The match and title depended on it. Deliberately and slowly she set herself for the all-important shot, and down went the putt surely into the centre of the can.

On that occasion is often centred an incident that highlights the great champion's intense concentration. The story goes:

On the 17th tee an appalled friend is said to have asked her, "Why didn't you wait until the train had passed. Didn't it upset you?"

"What train?" was the champion's classic reply.

At the 16th the railway line actually bordered the green and the trains trundled noisily past within ten yards of the flag. The clanking of the old steam 'puffers' heard hundreds of yards away, was generally the signal for anyone on the green to stay his putt until the train had passed from earshot. So wrapt in the putt ahead of her was Miss Wethered that she had been oblivious to all else.

Actually we have the authority of Lady Heathcote-Amory herself that while the incident is true, it actually happened at Sheringham a year or two earlier. In the 36-hole final she recalled that Glenna Collett was 34 out in "the finest sequence of holes I have ever seen a lady play". At that stage she had her opponent "five doon". Miss Wethered did the next 18 holes in 73, and from 5 down, stood 4 up at the 27th hole.

Almost as distinguished in amateur golf as his sister, Roger Wethered was an unlucky champion for whom the Old Course reserved one of its cruellest blows. The winning of the 1921 Open was in his grasp but for two blows of fate. Tragedy first stalked in when in his third round, he went forward, at the long 14th hole to survey the scene for his approach to the difficult green. Walking backwards, he inadvertently trod on his ball. He called attention to the incident and incurred a harsh penalty stroke.

Then, in his final round, Wethered dropped a shot by taking an inexplicable five at the par four last hole but still finished in 71. In the field still to come, only Jock Hutchison could beat him, provided he could shoot a 69. The St. Andrews-born professional returned a brilliant 70 to tie with the amateur, and then beat him handsomely in the replay. Thus began the first of the Trophy's many journeyings across the Atlantic, Hutchison, as a naturalised American being the first U.S. citizen to win it.

An unusual fact, and little known, is that throughout the championship, Wethered's caddie was 'Kail' Bell, a cousin of John Bell Hutchison, otherwise 'Jock', who beat the great amateur to the title!

A number of years ago, in 1957, St. Andrews was happy to see for the first and only time in action on the Old Course, the great American champion, Byron Nelson. Although he was past his best and did not seriously expect to win the title, he attracted a big following of the knowledgeable St. Andrews spectatorate, even in practice. At the 4th hole, as many long hitters have before him, 'King' Byron, in a reconnoitring round, found his ball from the tee sitting in the Cottage Bunker. He played a magnificent shot out of the trap and the few spectators watching saw his ball sail up to the green 110 yards away and land reasonably near the flag.

The parallel was too good to miss. Nelson's caddie told him, "That's the Cottage Bunker, where Bobby Jones played from almost the same lie as you, and holed it, in the 1930 Open."

Nelson looked at his ball, lying on the green for a safe par and a possible birdie, and turned to his caddie.

"Say," he drawled, "That's close enough for a practice round. Wait until tomorrow when the chips are down!"

The chips were down for Bobby Jones on that recalled occasion. It was the year 1930 when he was to achieve his unforgettable grand slam. In the first round of the Amateur, he met Sid Roper, a competent Nottingham golfer. At the first hole, Jones looked startled when he saw his 12-yard putt start off much too hard. But it hit the back of the can, bounced up and dropped in for a birdie. Another followed at the third. Then came his long drive into the Cottage Bunker at the fourth. From the depths of the trap he made the absolutely perfect recovery. His ball hit the green and ran into the hole for an eagle two!

Jones ended the championship by beating Roger Wethered by 7 and 6 in the final, to go one step nearer to achieving the quadruple championship feat that will probably never again be equalled.

The last hole of the Old Course with its wide fairways bounded by the road, and the packed terrace behind, is one of the greatest natural stages in the world. When Tony Lema won the 1964 Open Championship, a crowd of some 15,000 pressed behind him for his final shot to the green, while the same number waited, thronged around three sides of it. Lema had the title 'in his pocket' and the local gallery almost as much so, in admiration of his conquest of a course and conditions he had never encountered before. His long drive left him a short seventy or eighty yards from the green, but with the difficult Valley of Sin hollow to negotiate.

Lema, to the delight of the home crowd, elected to play the old St. Andrews run-up to the green, and did so to perfection. His shot ran up to four feet of the flag, and Lema downed it, with apparent calm, for a birdie to finish five strokes ahead of the burly Jack Nicklaus.

We say 'apparent' calm because already Lema, the handsome, ill-fated American, to use his own picturesque phraseology, was "away up on Cloud Nine'. He confirmed afterwards he was in a complete emotional daze as he stood on the historic green.

The close-pressing crowd was a record and the biggest since Hector Thomson's magnificent and spectacular approach which won for him the 1936 Amateur title, by beating burly Australian Jim Ferrier. That final was one which, for sheer drama, has been hard to match. Ferrier, at one point had been three up on the Scotsman in the morning round of the 36-hole final. Then he drove out of bounds over the wall at the long 14th. The match turned from that point with Thomson staging a magnificent recovery.

A tremendous crowd, the biggest ever seen at St. Andrews to that date, saw Thomson two up approaching the Road Hole green. A half was all he needed. His second lay near the foot of the green and

Ferrier had to go for the narrow hazard-bounded green. He played a wonder shot and won the hole in four. Thomson was now a hole up, with the Home Hole to play.

The crowds swarmed up both sides of the flat green rectangle formed by the 1st and 18th fairways, their caddies and the referee small and forlorn figures on their own in the arena. Every window-ledge and roof had its occupants and watchers clung precariously to chimney-pots. The two drives were up the middle. Ferrier played first, safely to the heart of the green. Could Thomson match it?

Henry Longhurst wrote:

"I see the ball now, flying high and white against the blue sky. It pitches on the short edge of the green, bounces once, twice, and there is a crescendo of roars, 'It's in, it's in'."

It wasn't in, but it was, as nearly as mattered, perhaps five inches from the hole. Ferrier with a wry smile, walked across the green to shake the new champion by the hand.

Could Britain for once win the Walker Cup? Two years later a tremendous crowd was again lining the last fairway watching Cecil Ewing and Ray Billows under the impression that on their match depended the result of the Cup. Ewing was one up and British hopes were high, with both on the green in two. Then, a roar from far out on the course. Alex Kyle, the Peebles man, had won his match and made the result secure. Britain had won! The atmosphere of drama dissipated at once from the scene on the last green. Everyone now took it for granted that big, bespectacled Ewing would get his four and win his match. Indifferently, now, they watched him, almost indifferently himself, hole out to win and increase Britain's winning margin.

The Cup for once had passed into British possession. It was not to happen again for 33 long, frustrating years.

The 1971 encounter was just as drama-packed, ending with Britain delighting the thronged spectators with a 13-11 victory.

Michael Bonallack's team fell behind in the early stages, but fought back to draw level at eleven-all with two matches still to come in. It was Roddy Carr, son of the Walker Cup veteran, Joe Carr, who had levelled the tally with a thrilling thirty-foot downhill putt on the Home Green to defeat James Simon. Then followed Scot George McGregor whose single-hole win over John Gabrielsen actually gave Britain the lead and sent home hopes soaring.

While he was sinking his vital winning putt, David Marsh just behind, was striding up the last fairway with a hole advantage over veteran Bill Hyndman. What matter that Hyndman levelled his match. Britain had won! Again, as 33 years earlier, the crowd gave vent to a full-throated roar of mad exuberance.

ADULATION

THE true St. Andrean, above all else, instinctively appreciates a good golfer. Local galleries at the Old Course watch and size-up with a dispassionately critical eye. All are cognoscenti, and there is no question of being 'fans' or of claques. Every competitor is judged on his merits as a player, and the top American, Australian or Japanese golfer gets the same impartiality of judgement as the home product.

Few golfing personalities have possessed sufficient magnetism or brilliance of play to stir the phlegmatic minds of the locals beyond that impartial appreciation, to the level of uncritical adulation or hero-worship. In 200 years of recorded golf only four men have achieved the idol's niche. Of these, two were not St. Andrews-born, but they became St. Andreans by popular adoption and acclaim.

For the man who is, by common consent, the greatest of these, let us go back to the Open Championship of 1921. A certain youthful Robert Tyre Jones is playing the short 11th hole in the course of his third round. At the end of 36 holes he is leading the amateurs. Disgustedly he surveys his ball lying deep in Hill Bunker, a fearsome sand-pit that is a terror to all who find it. Twice he attempts to blast his ball out of the hazard, but there the ball lies still.

Trying not at all well to bottle his emotions, Jones signals to his marker, tears up his card and walks off and out of the championship. On his own later admission, he hated the Old Course.

On to 1936. Bobby Jones . . . the affectionate diminutive is obligatory in St. Andrews . . . has carried all in golf before him six years earlier. He has achieved eternal golfing fame with the feat that will probably never again be emulated, of the 'Grand Slam'; to borrow Bernard Darwin's magniloquent phrase, 'the impregnable quadrilateral'. He has won all four major championships of Britain and America. By the disciplined way in which he had conquered himself and the Old Course, St. Andrews had taken him to its collective heart.

But Jones has retired from the game, laden with its honours, tired in spirit.

On a holiday trip to Britain and Europe to see the Olympic Games in Berlin, he suddenly decides he would like a quiet, friendly game at St. Andrews . . . a sentimental whim.

Until then his recent golf had been desultory and uninterested. Figures? . . . He doesn't even consider them. This game is to be merely a nostalgic round, a holiday relaxation. No publicity, no crowds. So, from Gleneagles Hotel, fifty miles away, a ballot for R. T. Jones and party was arranged.

That morning an electric thrill ran through St. Andrews. Bobby Jones was coming! As by extra-sensory perception the news spread. When Jones arrived at the first tee of the Old Course all St. Andrews was there to greet him. The few who could not make the starting time streaked round the course to make up on the game. The streets were deserted!

Never before had the town known a gesture so spontaneous. Bobby Jones could not but be touched, and he was, very deeply moved. Referring to the occasion, at another and even greater event 22 years afterwards, he said:

> "I have another great memory. In 1936 I set out with my wife to go to the Olympic Games in Berlin. Of course I took my clubs along because in those days they were very necessary impedimenta. We met friends and planned to stay two days at Gleneagles. We played rounds there. I told my friends I could not be this close to St. Andrews without making a pilgrimage to it. We got here about noon and had lunch. I had been playing perfectly dreadful golf, too, I can tell you. Anyway, we finished lunch and walked over to the first tee — and there were waiting over 2,000 people!

> "I said to myself. This is an awful thing to do to my friends if they have come to see me golf, with the dreadful stuff I am playing.

> "Anyway, Willie Auchterlonie and Gordon Lockhart (Gleneagles pro.) started off with me, but Gordon dropped off after two holes. By then the crowd had risen to over 4,000.

> "Such a spontaneous show of affection and warmth I have never known in my life. It was such a splendid welcome you people gave me that I played the best golf I had played for four

years, and certainly never since . . . I went out in 32 with a two at the eighth. I was so happy and in a transport almost that when I reached the 11th I went over 'Strath' going over the green and landed in a bunker that no longer exists. It was about 15 feet from the hole and I went out looking for it the other day (1958) and the greenkeeper told me it had never been there. I said to him, 'You can't tell me that, because I played two shots in it in 1936!'

'That was a great day for me."

For St. Andreans and for Bobby Jones an even greater day lay ahead, when he was presented with the freedom of St. Andrews.

It was not merely because he was so outstanding a golfer to be elevated by the Royal and Ancient Golf Club to the Corinthian designation of 'professional' that Allan Robertson (1815-1859) became the first golfing idol of St. Andrews and therefore of the world. A champion in the days before there was such an event as a championship, Allan was reckoned to be invincible when he wanted to win—when the stake money was there to be won. He had the particular quality and magnetism of the champion in full measure that he could exercise when needed.

Allan's powers as a golfer won him first the admiration and the respect of the aristocratic R. and A. members as he began to beat them all with almost contemptuous ease; then the glowing pride of his own artisan cronies, because, although he was one of themselves, he could beat the best. Within a few years, as they came to regard him as unbeatable, this pride soon swelled into outright hero-worship with the townspeople. His prestige rose higher as he was invited increasingly by the Club members to take part in their matches, and to teach them how to play better.

Robertson had his own Celtic brand of humour that was never far from the surface. Not tall, he had all the small man's confidence and assurance. On the course miracles were always expected of him, and he often produced miracles. He developed iron-play to an extent hitherto unknown. Until his day, the track-iron, made to dig balls out of rough lies, was the only known iron-headed club. For driving, pitching and putting, wooden clubs were used.

Allan not only improved the track iron, but he used it for running-up, and developed in into the cleek for that purpose. He was the

(Photo by G. M. Cowie)

Bobby Locke's Hour of Triumph—and Worry, 1957

The 'Big Three' in Colour TV Match, 1966

(Photo by G. M. Cowie)

originator of the St. Andrews run-up. He also devised a range of other irons for different purposes, but it was his personal wizardry in their use on the rough greens and rougher fairways that became the backbone of his invincible game.

The whole town of St. Andrews turned out when Allan was due to play a match. When it was a big-money encounter against champions from Musselburgh, Montrose, and Prestwick, the whole town backed him confidently, and they never lost their money. He never committed the grave sin to a Scotsman of developing a 'big head', or acting above his allotted station in life, despite his patronage by the R. and A.

Only Allan's partner and assistant in his business of ball-maker, Tom Morris, who was six years his junior, could approach him as a golfer. But Tom lacked the brittle, brilliant 'star' quality that Allan showed in abundance. A rare defeat for the champion was when Mr James Wolfe Murray, a prominent Club member, and a scion of the Scottish nobility, put up for the winner a new red coat in a straight challenge match between him and Tom Morris.

As usual, a large crowd turned out, with the sponsor a spectator to the match on his pony which he rode round the course. For once, Tom Morris was the winner, but it was Allan who gained the plaudits. Tongue in cheek, he said at the end of the game that all the way round he was thinking how much better the braw red coat would suit the stalwart figure of his opponent than his own small bulk!

It was not the only time that Morris beat him, but never in an important match. Allan had the habit, in minor games, of keeping a match going until near the end. Then he would turn to his partner and whisper: "We'll juist snod them at the 'Burn'." The Swilcan Burn was the 17th hole. A delightfully descriptive old Scots verb, to 'snod', unfortunately now obsolete.

"Who shall describe his elegant and beautifully correct style?" wrote one of the Club members, in a panegyric to the golfing hero of the time. "That easy style, depending on a long, cool swing, never on strength . . . In a word, his game is pure, unadulterated science. His short game, particularly his quarter shots, are accurate beyond belief . . . his deadly use of cleek up to the hole."

The "Dundee Advertiser", writing at the time of his death asked rhetorically: "Who that has once seen the champion golfer will ever forget him? Let us try to help the picture which every player will oft in fancy draw? Our scene is the St. Andrews Links on a genial summer day. Allan's house crowns the summit of the slope; down towards the sea . . . lies the white clubhouse, with its gravelled terrace. (The Union Parlour, prior to the present clubhouse.) . . . Down comes the champion in hot haste. He is dressed, as you must remember, in his favourite red jacket, and carries a cleek (a pet weapon) in his hand. But now the match is arranged. Allan has evidently got to nurse an elementary golfer. It is a foursome, Allan and his protégé against two rather good hands. Remark how pleasant the little man is; no miss of his partner causes a shade to his habitual good nature, and ten to one, when the match comes in from their round, the new player swears by 'Allan', and gives in his adhesion to golf once and for all."

So much for the first-ever idol of golf.

Most romantic of the idols of St. Andrews was 'Young Tommy', the eldest of the three sons of Tom Morris, and rather less than a generation after Robertson's era.

All the ingredients of a high Victorian melodrama were stirred into the brief days that comprise the plot of his life's story.

The golfing genius of Young Tom Morris coruscated from an early day. A world-beater at sixteen, he grew up tall, strong and incredibly handsome. A champion of champions, he was yet endearingly modest. But in the greatest days of his golfing triumphs, tragedy struck. He lost his beloved young wife and child in her first childbirth. He himself died soon after, "of a broken heart", at the age of 24 years.

But the hero-worship of Young Tommy was not a legend that swelled in retrospect as the result of his tragic life. He was idolised in his lifetime from the day when, at the age of sixteen, he beat all comers in a professional meeting at Carnoustie; then went up to Montrose and beat Willie Park of Musselburgh, the successor to Allan Robertson as the champion in Scotland.

"Whit hae ye brocht the laddie for, Tom?" said Park, when Tom Morris appeared at Carnoustie with his son.

"Ye'll ken whit for soon enough," calmly and prophetically replied Tom. The 'laddie' proceeded to beat both Park and his father along with the rest of the field, to win the money.

From that point Young Tom Morris embarked on an invincible career that continued until his death eight short years later. Mr Robert Clark, the contemporary R. and A. historian, described it as "The most brilliant display of golf ever known. He was the best player who ever addressed himself to a ball."

Only Davie Smith, a firm friend, could be described as a rival close enough to compare with him. An amiable temperament masked in Young Tom the determined concentration and 'killer instinct' of the true champion. He won the recently instituted Open Championship four times in a row. Probably the greatest of his four wins was in 1870 when he made the Championship Belt his own property by winning it for the third successive time. His two-round score of 149 meant that he had performed the unprecedented feat of twice breaking eighty, and his winning margin over the 36 holes was Olympian — eleven shots.

He was given a champion's reception in St. Andrews after this great feat, and again two years later in 1872 when he won the new championship trophy and had his name annexed as its first winner. The event had lapsed for a year while the R. and A. and the Prestwick Club, donors of the first Belt, were deciding about a new trophy. Part of Young Tommy's invincibility was his iron play which he had developed from the point where Allan Robertson had left off by using it for pitching. A niblick was his favourite weapon and he was the first golfer ever to learn how to impart back-spin to a ball and use it when he needed to.

Tragedy came swiftly. Something of the winning urge had gone from his play and he was not seen so much on the Links. Romance had come into his life and he married. In September, 1875, father and son went to North Berwick to play a challenge match against the Park brothers. The match was summarily stopped when a telegram arrived midway through telling of the death of his young wife and still-born child.

Only twice after did Young Tom play golf, on both occasions to honour engagements and as an attempt to stir him from his deadly lethargy. In the first, a foursome with his father against Davie Strath, his great friend, and Bob Martin, another St. Andrews professional the Morrises stood four up with five to play. Then Tommy completely broke down and threw away all five holes in a row. In his last match, he conceded a heavy handicap against the English amateur, Arthur Molesworth, but won over a frost-bound course. But his interest was perfunctory. Several days later, on Christmas morning, he was dead.

Mr Frederick Guthrie Tait, son of an Edinburgh professor, was known in St. Andrews just as "Freddie Tait". He possessed in abundance the epic quality that made him worshipped and lionised by the people of the town, by golfers generally and even, to some extent, by his fellow-members of the Royal and Ancient Golf Club. He, too, died young, killed by a Boer bullet in 1900 when he went to South Africa to fight for Queen and Country.

The son of a man who was one of the most enthusiastic golfers of his day, Freddie Tait became a member of the R. and A. in 1890. Both he and his father loved St. Andrews and all holidays were spent playing over the Old Course. The Professor's fanaticism for golf led him to propound a number of scientific theories on the game. One such, his son very thoroughly scotched in 1892 after the Professor had come to the conclusion that a golf ball could only be hit to carry a maximum distance of 190 yards. Playing the 13th hole of the Old Course, young Freddie drove a gutta ball to within ten yards of the greenside bunker . . . a distance of 341 yards nine inches, solemnly measured immediately afterwards, and fully authenticated in every way. It carried 250 yards!

F. G. Tait attracted the golfing galleries like a magnet. He first came into the limelight in 1893 when he beat Harold Hilton, the famous English amateur and favourite for the Amateur title. A report of the game said: "Mr Tait's stupendous driving is becoming a household word wherever golf is spoken."

He revelled in the cut-and-thrust of match play and the rapidly growing galleries of the time loved him for it, and for his high spirits. He was an enthusiastic piper and Andrew Lang, the Scottish poet and historian, wrote of him: "You never heard a word said against him except a solitary complaint that, in the lightness of his heart, he played pibrochs round the drowsy town at the midnight hour." But

Tait hated the publicity that his prowess attracted. He loved St. Andrews, but wherever he played, sooner or later he lowered the course record. On the Old he won every possible R. and A. award and many other trophies, as well as twice being amateur champion. Twice also he won the St. George's Vase at Sandwich, one of the country's leading amateur awards. In the same year that he joined the R. and A. he lowered the Old Course record with a score of 77, then reduced it to a phenomenal 72 four years later.

In 1897 he was third in the Open Championship, and first in the amateur. In the following year he finished fifth and was again first amateur, although his dislike of medal play was genuine. He described it as "a dull spiritless exercise, like rifle shooting." Tait was the ideal match player, with no quarter asked, and none given. In winning his first amateur title, he played round after round of devastating golf. He beat one champion-to-be and four former champions on his way to the final. In that round he defeated the favourite, Harold Hilton, by a formidable 8 and 7.

Tait once played the North Berwick professional, Ben Sayers, on his own course and beat him by 8 holes. Afterwards, "Wee Ben" was heard to say incredulously, "On my own green, by an amateur! It's no possible, but it's a fact!"

In the South African War, Lt. Tait went with his regiment, the famous Black Watch, into battle, and he died in battle. The news of his death in 1900 was received with the desolate sense of personal loss and deepest sorrow in St. Andrews that had greeted the passing of Young Tom Morris twenty-five years earlier. He was mourned everywhere that golf was played.

A memorial that touched and pleased the citizens was the lovely gold medal, with its Black Watch ribbon, that his family presented to the city as a trophy for the local championship of the Links. Appropriately, it was decided that it must be a match-play event. It is the most highly regarded of local trophies, played for traditionally over the New Course each year.

The Golf Club of Kimberley for many years has undertaken the duty of looking after Tait's grave at Koodoosberg, and a Tait Cup is given annually to the best South African amateur in their Open Championship.

No words better describe Freddie Tait and the historic grey old city he loved than Andrew Lang's tribute on his death:

"I stop to gaze across the glooming flats of the sodden links, and seem to see again him who is now but the brightest of the shadows that haunt this place of many memories. Bruce and Wallace, Culdees and grim Covenanters, the frail wandering ghost of the exiled Henry VI; Knox in his vigour and Knox in his decline; the stern Regent Moray, and the harmless Lyon King-at-Arms whom he burned; they are all among our haunting shades, with the Queen (Mary, Queen of Scots) in her glad youth, and Chastelard, here condemned to die for her, and her French valet in like case, and the great Cardinal in his glory, and the anxious eyes of Mariotte Ogilvy, and Montrose in his boyhood — a thousand characters of immortal memory, with the same shroud around them all. But he who died in Africa, glad and kind as he was brave till his latest breath — he, too, will not be forgotten." Koodoosberg Drift. 1900.

CADDIES' CANTRIPS

THE TROTTING CLUB-MAN

It is indeed a goodly sight to see
Those red-coat champions marshalled for the fray,
Driving the ball o'er bunker, rut and lea,
And clearing with imperious 'fore' the way,
Enlivening still the game with laugh and say,
Whilst trotting club-man follows fast behind
Prepared with ready hand and tees to lay,
With nicest eye the devious ball to find,
And of the going game each player to remind.

It is in sooth a goodly sight to see,
By east and west, the Swilcan lasses clean,
Spreading their clothes upon the daisied lea,
And skelping freely barefoot o'er the green,
With petticoats high kilted up I ween,
And note of jocund ribaldry most meet,
From washing tubs their glowing limbs are seen
Veiled in an upward shower of dewy weet,
Oh, 'tis enough to charge an anchorite with heat!

BLACKWOOD'S, Sept., 1819.

"The trotting club-man who follows fast behind", in the verse, was the caddie of some two hundred years ago. The second verse refers to another ancient right of St. Andrews citizens vested in the Links that was exercised up to as recently as a century ago—namely of the townspeople to wash and bleach their clothes on the sward in the vicinity of the Swilcan Burn. As a freeman of the City, Bobby Jones enjoyed that right. A special rule was made as late as 1857 for any ball that should land on the clothes drying and bleaching on the green at the side of the fairway. It could be lifted without penalty!

The traditional St. Andrews caddie, from whom sprang the original professionals of the game, has always taken his duties with the seriousness due to gowff. He was not a mere porter, or carrier of clubs; he was an expert in the game. He often fought and bled for victory for his employer—his man! He agonised over every stroke played and he tendered advice. He and his 'man' were a team. That is still true. Tony Lema, the effervescent American professional, who died so tragically in 1966, had the temerity to play over the Old Course in the Open Championship of 1964 with only scant practice rounds. He had the greater audacity to win it.

Lema paid handsome tribute to his St. Andrews born and bred caddie, 'Tip' Anderson, Jr., son of 'Tip', also a caddie. Lema declared that without him he could never have won the title. The Andersons, father and son, were in the line of traditional St. Andrews caddies, and it is worthy of note that 'Young Tip', as he is known, was himself a golfer of considerable merit, and has caddied for years for Arnold Palmer in Britain. In the same line was the late Wallace Gillespie, who in 1955 brought home Peter Thomson, the Australian star, as winner on the Old Course of the Open. There are few of the top professionals who can 'read' the course as Thomson does, and much of his knowledge came from Gillespie.

Of 'Tip', Lema said: "He was far more useful to me than a club. Without his help I doubt if I could have won it. It amazed me the way he just put the club in my hand."

A rather different story from that of a disgruntled Sam Snead in 1946 when he arrived at the last minute to find all the recognised caddies were booked, and condemned all local caddies from the dregs he was left to suffer.

But it is a dying race thanks largely to the wider range of employment that a much more industrialised Scotland can now offer her people. In former days, work in and around the small seaside towns which possessed links for golf courses was limited. Employment was a survival of the fittest, mentally and physically. Caddies often were drawn from those who had failed in the struggle, although in the early days the best type was the boy or young man who had become a greenkeeper, clubmaker or ballmaker. A great part of the duties of Tom Morris, for instance, in his earlier days, consisted of acting as caddie for one or other of the members of the R. and A. when he was not partnering them in a wager match. Before him Allan Robertson, the first professional, also caddied often. After him so did Andra Kirkaldy.

For the rest, the caddies were odd-job men. They took on their humble role with matter-of-fact acceptance, and from the interest they generally took in the game, derived a tremendous vicarious enjoyment, through the efforts of their employer of the moment . . . their 'man'. The good caddie became the player. He tendered advice, watched his 'man's' ball like a hawk to make sure it was never lost, and was always ready with a stentorian and officious cry of 'fore' to see that his player got a clear field of play. Up to 1854, their warning cry was "Cut your stick and look sharp!"

An intimate companionship and *rapport* was often established between the player and his caddie in this way, and the more patrician the player, the more he generally strove to achieve that relationship. Many of the top tournament golfers, amateur and professional, still try to establish that same communion with their regular caddies, not so much nowadays for advice, but as a rampart in that wall of concentration they have to build against the surrounding galleries that besiege them on the course. The caddie, of course, is recognised by the rules as part of the side, and as such, can involve his player in penalty for infringement.

The word 'caddie' comes simply from the French 'cadet' meaning a little chief. It was applied around 1700 by Scottish irony to street loafers who were ready to run errands or do odd jobs; it came to mean a porter, and, naturally, the Gentlemen golfers quickly applied it to the men who carried their clubs for them. Caddies are almost as old as the game and were regularly employed by royalty and the nobility on the links, as for instance, Mary Queen of Scots in the 1500s, James II, Charles I, etc. Generally their man-servants acted as their caddies. The caddie was merely 'the boy who carried my Lord's clubbes to the fields', as he was described in the household accounts of the Marquis of Montrose in 1628.

In St. Andrews a caddie undertakes not to caddie, but to 'carry' and still does. There is no verb 'to caddie'. To illustrate, the prime example is the famous retort of the Old Course caddie whose 'man' had left a jacket behind and wanted his caddie to go to the clubhouse and fetch it. He was promptly told: "Go back for it yersel'. I'm paid to carry—no' to fetch and carry!"

In St. Andrews the unusual relationship between master and caddie often developed to an extraordinary extent. In fact, most members of the R. and A. up to the First World War had their own regular caddies and took a deep interest in their welfare. The social conscience of the Club was even officially roused to attempt to improve their lot. In May, 1863, the possibility of opening an evening school for younger boys was considered, and seven years later the rules were tightened up, so that no boy under seven was to be allowed to carry clubs. Boy-caddies up to the age of 18 had to continue their education and attend a Sunday School. They were not to use bad language, and were supplied with a cap bearing the club badge, which they were compelled to wear on the Links. A Club Committee whose duty was to confer with the School Board on the matter of evening classes, was appointed also in 1873. A caddies' benefit fund was established as well, and a shelter built for them, largely through the good offices of some St. Andrews ladies. Nicholas Robb, previously a coastguard at Crail, was appointed the first caddie-master at £60 per year.

In 1863 it was considered fair that a caddie should get £1 for his services during the May or Autumn meetings, then lasting a week, or 1/6 for a first round and 6d for a second. This applied to caddies over 20 years of age. These younger got 15/- for a whole meeting or 1/- for the first round and 6d for the second. Each caddie had to have a ticket to show he was on the list, and pay 2/6 deposit at the beginning of the season. At the end of the year, after damages to the caddie shelter had been paid for, the Club doubled the money left over, and the whole sum was divided among the caddies who had a clean sheet. Clothing was provided for those in need out of a special fund.

These provisions were decades in advance of industrial and social welfare of the times, and were an indication of the personal relationship between 'man' and caddie. The regular members of the Club over the years, had their special caddies. Mr Hope Grant would have been lost without Sandy Pirie. Sandy Herd's grandfather was the inseparable henchman of John Whyte-Melville, who for 70 years played two rounds of golf a day, three days of the week throughout the year. Old Bob Kirk always carried for Campbell of Saddell, while 'Andra' Strath was the only caddie for old Sutherland, after whom a bunker on the Old Course is named. The professionals also had their favourite carriers. Allan Robertson always had Davie Anderson, Tom Morris had Bob Kirk, and so on.

The greatest 'character' among the caddies of the emergent days was 'Lang Willie'. His garb for years was a tall hat, swallowtailed coat and light trousers. Although he got drunk regularly, Willie insisted that he drank nothing but sweet milk. He once fell completely out of patience with one of the university professors and told him: "It's easy work learning thae laddies at the college Latin and Greek, but when you come to play golf, you man hae a head!"

Later, there were 'Poot' Chisholm, Donald Blue, and a whole host of others, all eccentrics or 'characters' as they were called, peculiarities due almost entirely to their narrow, parochial and illiterate upbringing.

Davie Robertson, father of Allan, was the senior caddie of his day, although the family had been the traditional ballmakers in St. Andrews for generations, and that was his chief occupation. Allan's remarkable prowess as a player raised the status of professional beyond that of superior caddie, but just beyond. It was not until Henry Cotton came along a century later that the next significant jump up the social ladder came for the British professional.

Lord Brabazon recorded that when, in 1949 he took the first caddie car round the Old Course, he caused consternation among the caddies waiting at the time. There is no doubt that their introduction did reduce the demand on the services of caddies, and it was not very long after that the services of a caddie-master for the Links were dispensed with as unnecessary. The old type of caddie is dying out, largely due to improving social conditions, but the race is not quite extinct. The present day caddies are probably less of 'characters', but generally, excellent at their job. The services of a real St. Andrews caddie is still part of the experience to be enjoyed by any visitor who wants to recapture something of the traditional *ethos* of the game in its traditional home. The Links Trust has now restored the caddie-master to the golfing scene.

Not surprisingly, in view of their hard circumstances and stern environment, the wit of the St. Andrews caddie has always been mordant and pungent, although ever-present and unquenchable. A tradition among them was that a 'foreigner' — any caddie from outside the town, had to give up his first fee and have his health drunk in the caddie shelter. Occasionally, this was a prelude to a celebration and a caddie would take to the course somewhat the worse. Old Grant was told by his 'man': "You're drunk; I won't have a drunk caddie."

Scathingly came the reply. "Mebbe I am drunk, but I'll get sober. You canna gowff and you'll never get better." And off he staggered, scattering his 'man's' clubs around on the ground. (In those days they were carried loose under their arms by the caddies. The first bag did not come along until Dr Traill's canvas container appeared on the Old Course about 1890.)

The grandfather of Sandy Herd, of the same name, had an equally withering retort for a very wealthy R. and A. member who presented him with a tip of 2d.

"Are ye sure ye can spare it, sir?" he asked sarcastically. "I'll no' miss it!"

In the early stages of the game's popularity, when big money matches between the professionals of different areas were attracting increasingly large galleries of spectators, partisanship among the onlookers ran high on certain courses. Often, spectators' money was also at stake. Their conduct frequently far transgressed the etiquette of golf as devised by the Society of Golfers in their Corinthian days, when sportsmanship was all.

The St. Andrews caddies, reared in these traditions, took badly with the bias of the spectators, shown in various ways. Carrying for Bob Martin, an Open Champion, at a course in the west of Scotland, Tam Chisholm turned on a gallery that was being vocally partial.

"Think shame on ye," Tam shouted. "Booin' and cheerin' like that. Wad ye dae that in the kirk?"

When Rex Hartley, the English Walker Cup player of the '30s won the Silver Tassie at Gleneagles, he took up his St. Andrews caddie to carry for him. Near the end, with a good chance of winning in sight, he asked for a spoon for one shot, saying he could get nicely home with a shot cut into the wind.

The caddie was for none of these fancy shots. "Ye'll tak your iron, and hit it straight," he said. "Whit dae ye think ye're playing in! A pantomime?"

Hartley took the iron, played as required and won the Tassie.

Another caddie had been at a concert the night before when among the items was a rendering of the poem "The Charge of the

Light Brigade", which includes the lines: 'Their's not to reason why; their's but to do or die, Into the valley of Hell, rode the Six Hundred'.

His 'man' the next day was a somewhat timid R. and A. member who was extra anxious to win his match.

"Jist you leave it tae me," said Donald. "I'll tell ye whit tae dae and whit tae play."

They were getting on reasonably well and at the 16th hole Donald's man stood one up. He duly drove well to the left as instructed, but, when it came to his chip shot when still short in two, Donald told him: "Noo, jist you run it up wi' this," and handed over a straight-faced club. "And run it ower that bump." The bump in question was several yards off the line and the player expostulated.

In a fury, Donald turned on him. "Your's not to reason why," he intoned from the previous night's poem. Then he added with an intimidating snarl: "Your's but tae dae whit you're bluidy well telt!"

The shot was duly played as demanded, and almost holed, a four being good enough to win the hole and the match.

Warren Wind, the noted American golf writer, recorded from his experience: The old St. Andrews caddie does not butter up his man, but there is no limit to his resourcefulness in reading the course for his man. In the 1950 Amateur Willie Turnesa hooked his tee shot far off line on the par four 7th hole. The ball landed at the base of the abrupt rise that shuts off all view of the fairway and the green beyond. Turnesa's caddie studied the situation for a moment, handed him his No. 5 iron, and, pointing to the sky, said drily, "Juist hit that cloud." Turnesa duly 'hit the cloud' and found his ball six feet from the cup!

"The golfer who does not take a caddie at St. Andrews denies himself the wine of the country," added Wind. He recalled that Laurence Buddo Gourlay taught King Edward VII and the Grand Duke Michael of Russia how to play the game at Cannes, and in the 1920s became the special caddie of the Prince of Wales who played himself in as Captain of the R. and A.

Typical of the caddie who regarded himself as an expert and as his man's overlord is the story of one such at the famous short 11th hole. He handed his man his No. 4 iron only after some deliberation. His employer duly addressed the ball and had reached the top of his swing when he was halted by the caddie's frantic cry. "Stoap! Stoap! I've decided to play the shot wi' oor spoon!"

In support of the caddie's opinion of his importance in the partnership, it was a St. Andrews caddie, Duncan, who won the 1923 Walker Cup for America.

Duncan was carrying for Dr Willing and the score stood at five matches all. Willing and his opponent, W. A. Murray, were all square at the Road Hole. The American's second shot lay short of the green and to the left . . . a dangerous position and a tremendously difficult approach to the green which falls away into a deep and narrow bunker. The flag was just at the top of the rise. Duncan studied the position carefully, and then he showed his man the exact line to the hole with a run-up shot. All credit to Dr Willing that he took the line given to him and then played the exact strength of shot. The ball ran its circuitous route to lie dead for a winning four, to give Willing the verdict by 2 and 1.

Referring to the last round of golf he played on the Old Course in 1936, Bobby Jones in "Golf Is My Game", wrote: "On the 8th tee I was paid the most sincere compliment I can remember ever. It was one of those things one does not talk about. The pin at the 8th was tucked behind a small mound to the right of the usual pathway leading to the front of the green. Having the honour I played a short shot with a No. 4 iron. As I stepped back, my caddie, a pleasant young man of about twenty years said to me under his breath. "My, but you're a wonder, sir." I could only smile and pat him on the shoulder. I do not know his name or where he is, but I hope he will now understand what pleasure he gave me."

Stories about Andra Kirkaldy who came out of the caddie ranks and often carried in his earlier days, and his caustic, rough-and-ready wit with prince and commoner, are legion. A good story-teller himself, in his pungent and graphic way, he has subsequently had many of them ascribed to himself.

Kirkaldy was getting an unusually stiff match from a lesser St. Andrews professional, Andrew Scott, with a fairish sum at stake. However, he sank a good putt at the 16th to become dormy.

Picking his ball out of the hole, he turned to his opponent and growled in his most intimidating manner. "That's the door lockit noo, Scott!"

One golfer trapped in Hell Bunker, after going through the range of his clubs in trying to extricate his ball, asked him, "What should I do now?"

"If I were ye," replied Andra, "I'd tak the 9.40 train oot o' St. Andrews."

In similar vein, it is told of him, when asked by a particularly poor player which line he should take at the 16th, Andra told him dryly, "I'd tak' the North British, if I were you." (One of the competing railway lines of the time.)

Celebrities in all walks of life have long come to St. Andrews to golf. A former Bishop of London clambered out of Hell Bunker beaming to his caddie. "That was a good recovery, caddie," he said, after a shot out of the famous hazard. "Aye," retorted his caddie, caustically, "When ye dee, mind and tak' your niblick wi' ye!"

On another occasion the Bishop, after being told the line was "yon mansion", skied his shot. "I didna' say, heavenly mansion," grunted Kirkaldy.

A. J. Balfour, former Prime Minister of Britain, was as keen a golfer as later was President Eisenhower. He came to St. Andrews as often as possible. One of the largest galleries for such an occasion saw him make the ceremonial drive that made him Captain of the R. and A. in 1894.

One caddie was boasting to his man, a casual visitor, about his friendship with various noted personalities, and claimed a very close relationship with Mr Balfour. This was received with scepticism by his man, and the caddie indignantly snorted: "I should ken him well, and I dae. I'm wearing his breeks!" (trousers).

Another local caddie, commenting on the same Prime Minister as a golfer, remarked: "Aye, wi' his height an' my brains, we'd mak a grand foursome."

One of the County Court justices was on the bench when young Robbie Black was called as a witness. "Do you understand the nature of an oath?" gravely asked his Honour. "Oh aye, sir," answered Robbie, with equal gravity. "I've carried your clubs mony a time."

Tam Chisholm, a somewhat disreputably dressed caddie, was asked to carry for a lady who had a camera with her. She asked Tam if he would mind her taking his photograph. Some days later she brought him the result. "Is this me?" asked Tam. She nodded. "Is it like me?" Again she nodded. "Aweel" said Tam gravely, "it's a humblin' sicht!"

"I'm playing Major Grundy tomorrow," said one member of the Club to his caddie, "What sort of player is he?" "Him, he canna play worth a damn," said Wullie. "He's nae better than yersel'."

Another player who was not doing well asked his caddie, "Do you think anybody could play worse than I've been doing?" "Weel," said his caddie after due deliberation. "There may be worse players, but it's likely they dinna try to play golf."

Some of the undiplomatic comments of local caddies can be nerve-shattering at times.

A certain Mr Robert Gourlay was a fanatic of golf, but to say he was a poor player was flattering him. The caddies generally avoided him, and it was no surprise when a newcomer to the caddie lists found he was carrying for him.

At the end of a terrible round, Mr Gourlay said apologetically to his caddie: "I don't suppose you've ever seen a worse player than me?"

His caddie cheerily replied: "No, I havena', but they tell me there is a worse. They say wee Bobby Gourlay's the worst player on the Links!"

Gourlay had a sense of humour. He often told this against himself.

Another caddie was congratulated by the minister of one of the local churches on having appeared at a special service the night before.

"Oh, that's whaur I got tae, was it?" bleakly commented the blear-eyed bag carrier.

(Photo by permission of Mrs D. J. B. Ritchie)

Swilcan Burn guarding 1st Green

(Photo by permission of Mrs D. J. B. Ritchie)

Hell Bunker at notorious long 14th

(Photo by G. M. Cowie)

The Black Sheds at Road Hole before demolition, 1967

A very impatient golfer stood on the second tee of the Old. "Can I play now, caddie?" he asked, as the pair ahead played their seconds. "Ye can gang ahead now" said his caddie. "But" he muttered for his own satisfaction, "Ye canna play!"

After his first round on the Old Course, the visitor picked up his ball on the Tom Morris green. "This is an awful course for bunkers" he told his caddie. "Aye," said old Lewis Rodger. "And there's twa or three mair that ye havena been in."

Professor T—— of the University, took up the game when he came to the city. "How's he getting on?" a friend asked the professor's usual caddie. "Yon man wull never mak a gowfer," declared the caddie. "When he foozles, a' he says is 'tut-tut'."

A former resident of the city achieved considerable fame as a barrister. During a holiday he employed a caddie whom he had known as a boy. "Ye're daein' weel at the Bar, I'm telt" said his caddie. "Not so badly," he replied with smiling satisfaction. "Aweel," said Anderson, his caddie, "I think you should stick to that and gie up the gowf."

A local lady, playing over the Eden Course, was annoyed at the slow gait of her caddie. Looking down, she saw his boots were several sizes too big for him, and remarked, "These are monstrous boots you've got on." "Yes, ma leddy," he replied, "They're your husband's auld anes!"

At the end of the game, the caddies were waiting while their men totted up their score cards. One was being very long about it. "He doesna' seem able to coont," remarked one. "I'm sure that's no' the trouble," was the reply. "I've been carrying for him for a week, and he's never once gi'en me a penny ower muckle."

On the same theme of counting, one caddie had suspicions about his man's opponent. At the end, he announced, to no one in particular, "Coonting coonts as much as playing."

A visitor to the Old was revelling in playing above himself. He was delighted with some of his shots, but his caddie never uttered a word of praise. Finally, at the Road Hole, he laid his second dead, a magnificent shot to that tricky green. "What do you think of that?" he asked his caddie delightedly. "It'll dae" was the calm and dampening reply.

The annual match of the R. and A. against the Town is the event of the year for some of the town worthies, as they have the hospitality of the Clubhouse at the end of their match. Tammy was a guest of Sir David, an important member who plied him with whisky. "Are you enjoying your drink, Tammy?" asked his host. "Aye, sir, I am that, but I'm missing ma glass o' beer." "Well, have a glass of beer, too" said Sir David.

"What! drink beer when you're peying, Sir David? No' blooming likely!"

As a commentary on brains against brawn, the following is one of the most crushing:

The day was windy, even for St. Andrews. It was a needle match between two R. and A. members. Lord W—— playing cannily into the wind, with a half-swing and slightly shut faced club, was keeping his ball low and straight. His opponent, Col. M——, a long hitter, but erratic, was playing in his usual manner, and his ball was all over the course. By the 12th he was 6 down and the match practically over, as the Colonel's drive sliced once more far into the whin. "Well, I doubt that's it, Rodger," he said dolefully to his veteran caddie. "I couldn't keep them straight." "Aye, Colonel," replied old Lewis drily, "No like his Lordship. He's no' playing a proud game."

COURSE FOR CONNOISSEURS

"In my humble opinion, St. Andrews is the most fascinating golf course I have ever played. . . . There is always a way at St. Andrews, although it is not always the obvious way, and in trying to find it, there is more to be learned on this British course than in playing 100 ordinary American golf courses."

BOBBY JONES.

THE world's best golfers of the last hundred years and more are among the countless players who have made ritual pilgrimages to the Mecca of Golf in order to play over the Old Course.

Some of these visitors, initially have been disappointed, have felt let down.

And, at first introduction, the Old Lady looks dowdy and hopelessly old-fashioned to those accustomed to the sophisticated country club atmosphere. But the better the player and the longer the acquaintance, the more deeply he falls victim to her wiles and subtle fascination.

American title-hunt invaders find they have to adjust themselves to a much different concept of golf from their artificially planned and carefully manicured circuits in the layout of which any element of chance is anathema.

The traditional Scottish concept is described by Robert Chambers in his "Golfing". It reflected the basic principles and rules of the early societies of golfers in Scotland. He said: "Those Links which possess no hazards are considered inferior to those on which they plentifully occur. . . : The avoidance of hazards constitutes much of the superiority of an excellent player." (The hazards on the Old and the other original seaside links were of course all natural—sand-pits, heather, whin and the elements.)

Bob Gardner, the distinguished American amateur and Walker Cup captain, in 1926, had the following to say after his team's win over the Old that year:

> "After one round I thought the Old Course was the worst I had ever known. On my second visit I played three rounds and ended by thinking it was quite a good course, after all. On the third occasion I played there for a week and ended by concluding it was the most wonderful course in the world."

The finest golfer in the world of his day, Bobby Jones, paid the most handsome and the most thoughtful tribute of all, after having had similar sentiments to Gardner on his first introduction to the course in 1921. It was a chastening experience for him, and he had hard things to say and even harder thoughts at first. But let us recall his own reminiscences on that often-reported incident to a St. Andrews audience 37 years afterwards:

> "I would like you to know I did not say a lot of the things that were put out I said. *But I could not play the course, and I did not think anyone else could.* I ask you to remember, of course, that I had attained the ripe old age of 19 years, and I did not know much about golf. Actually, that first time, we got along pretty good, the Old Course and I for two rounds. I scored 151. Of course, the wind was not blowing. But I started off in the third round and the wind was blowing in my face. That day it was really blowing. I reached the turn in 43 and when I was playing the 7th, 8th and 9th, I thought, 'Well, that's fine, I'll be blowing home with the wind'."

> "Well, as I stood on the 10th tee it turned right round and it blew all the way home against me. I got a six at the 10th and then put my iron into Hill Bunker, not Strath, as they said. They also say that when I got out of that bunker I hit my ball right into the Eden. That's not so, for I never did get the ball out of Hill Bunker!"

Later in his playing career, when full of triumphs, Jones could say:

> "In my humble opinion St. Andrews is the most fascinating golf course I have ever played . . ."

On another occasion he wrote: "St. Andrews changes with the wind, and the wind bloweth where and when it listeth. It may follow you all round the course, out and in, or it may oppose you all the way, turning when you turn. And, again, it may come across from the right, or the left, constantly, or with a baffling intensity."

In 1950 Jones, in an interview spoke these simple, final words: "*If I had ever been set down in any one place and told I was to play there, and nowhere else for the rest of my life, I should have chosen the Old Course.*"

These words show something of the depth of his affection for the Links of St. Andrews. No one has ever been taken with warmer and deeper esteem into the hearts of its custodians, the citizens of St. Andrews.

Gene Sarazen, describing the Old as undoubtedly the finest golf course in the world, said: "I wish that every man who plays golf should play at St. Andrews once." Yet Sarazen had, like Jones, chastening experiences on the Old.

George Duncan: "Unhesitatingly, the Old Course of St. Andrews is my favourite. I think it is the best and when I had to play a match of importance that was where I wanted to play it. St. Andrews has character and features that you get nowhere else. What I like about it is that you may play a very good shot there and find yourself in a very bad place. That is a real game of golf."

Australian Peter Thomson, winner of the Open five times, has also repeatedly given it as his considered view that the Old is the best in the world. That view is shared by many other 'greats'.

Yet occasionally the reaction has been that of Sam Snead when he duly arrived for practice for the 1946 Open. He took one look at the bare, featureless expanse before him, with its tiny starter's box, and was all for turning back. Recalling he was on business, and none has the reputation of paying more heed to business than Snead, he stayed on, and won the title with a score of 290.

Above all, the Old Course is a stern test of temperament, and the players, men or women, with the imperturbable resilient temperament, are those who win her favours.

The visiting player must try to see the Old Course as it is . . . an area of links land where golf has been played endlessly for nigh on a thousand years; whose original plan was shaped largely by nature and has stood the test of all that time. Nature's master plan has produced 18 holes that all possess their own character and individuality. That plan includes the simplest of ingredients; smooth, close-cropped turf, heather moorland and dense whin or gorse; a few big sand-pits, such as Hell, the Cottage and Shell bunkers that are older far than the Course.

The Old has proved itself capable of being moulded to suit each and every of the major developments of golf that have arrived. It will always do again for any developments that may lie ahead.

PLUS LA MEME CHOSE

In the passage of time a number of slight changes has inevitably been made on the Old Course without altering the layout in any way. Bunkers have been added, others taken away, but only after the weightiest deliberation. The Old Course is a treasured heritage and cared for as such.

Greens and fairways over the past century have been widened. They were hewn out of clinging heather and the dense, encircling Scottish whin that is as uncompromising as the essential national character, but whose bloom dazzles like the sun over the Links on a brilliant summer's day.

Two major changes only have ever been introduced to the natural layout that just evolved as part of the development of the game. The first was as late as 1832 when the expedient of doubling the size of some of the greens was resorted to in order to accommodate the steadily increasing number of players comprising the Society of Golfers.

The second alteration, comparatively slight though it is, was the most revolutionary change that the Old Course has ever undergone. It was the creation of a new first green; a case of the 'first' being last — the last to be laid down. Previously the present 17th had served as 1st and 17th greens.

The new surface, created in 1870, was therefore the means of instituting the possibility of playing the Old in two ways — the old left-hand course used since double greens were made in 1832 — and a new (the present) right-hand circuit. Each method had its protagonists and its own attractions. The right-hand won and has become customary ever since.

On occasion the left-hand course is used in winter to rest overworked areas, but the superiority of the right-hand in the general estimation is proved by the fact that only once since 1870 was the left-hand course ever used for a championship. This was in 1886, and was due entirely to an administrative oversight. Tom Morris was then responsible for the alternating rota. It happened to be the week of the left-hand, and the fact of the Open being played was forgotten about! The competitors started by playing the course left-hand, and so it continued to the end of the 1886 event.

The new 1st green has passed its centenary, and can be reckoned now to be settling down nicely!

A brief account of other changes and improvements in the Course is not out of place. Prior to 1832 the original breadth of the fairways, unchanged for centuries until then, was less than one-third of the present course. All that was considered needful was a narrow track of clear ground for playing out a number of holes and then back-tracking over them. Doubling the size of the greens also necessitated widening the fairways to a similar extent.

Appropriately, that most revolutionary alteration in the age-old history of the course was brought largely about by the man who was responsible for revolutionising St. Andrews itself. He was Sir Hugh Lyon Playfair, who around the early 1850s, instituted sweeping changes in the city, by clearing out many of its insanitary buildings. He modernised it up to the standards of a health resort acceptable to the growing band of middle-class golfing acolytes and their families. Sir Hugh was Provost (Mayor) of St. Andrews, a former captain of the Royal and Ancient Golf Club and one of its most staunch members. He was a forthright and at times, eccentric character. He had a fine tombstone erected in the town churchyard some years before his death. Another foible was to have inserted on his umbrellas "Stolen from Major Playfair". He was never seen without his "lum" hat, the kind used as a measure for stuffing featheries.

Playfair's good work of land reclamation in the area of the present 18th fairway of the Old was later continued and extended by George Bruce, another enterprising and forward-looking individualist, who recovered from the sea the lovely stretch of green sward known as the Bruce Embankment.

The 1st fairway, before this reclamation, was only about 80 yards in width. Sand from the sea was blown up as far as the steps leading up to the Clubhouse from the green. Gravel was occasionally washed up as close as a few yards away from the hole. Players teed up two club lengths from the last hole for their opening drives because there was little more space than that available to them to do so. Grannie Clark's Wynd, the road that bisects the 1st and 18th fairways, was simply a sandy track down to the beach, and some yards beyond it was Halket's Bunker, long-since filled up. The Swilcan Burn meandered across the course, a sandy-edged hazard. Sand for a player's tee was taken from the bottom of the hole. This was the reason why the holes often became so deep that it was difficult to scoop the ball out at times, after holing out.

Mr W. T. Linskill, the Englishman who founded Cambridge University Golf Club, and whose love of golf decided him to settle in St. Andrews, recalled in 1906 that between the Clubhouse and the Swilcan many acres of land were reclaimed from the sea.

> "Where I can remember the sea-shore once existed, there are now excellent lies for the players' balls. There are, I believe, three sea walls buried under the 'golf-green' (*i.e.*, the course), and the old bathing place was once under the present window of the north room of the Club. The historic Swilcan Burn formerly swept almost into the centre of the Links before it turned into the sea, and one often drove into this bed from the first tee. It was then a sandy natural hazard, but now it is a concrete-walled channel."

After Playfair had made the first sea-barrier on what is now the first fairway, he had grass sown, which was largely paid for by the old Union Club, the rival club which the R. and A. later absorbed. Later, George Bruce, at his own expense, made his further spectacular reclamation of the Embankment. He bought four fishing boats, placed them in a row, bow to stern, roughly at the point where the shelter on the Bruce Embankment now stands, roped them together, and half-filled them with concrete. On top of that he piled heavy stones. On the east side of the boats a sloping barricade of stakes was driven into the foreshore. The Town Council then used the area behind this barricade as a refuse dump.

When the boats were washed out of position by any unusually strong sea, Bruce persistently replaced them time after time. In front of the line of the dunes farther out, marram grass was sown along with ryegrass and later on lupins were introduced. Little by little, valuable ground in that area was reclaimed, to the immense benefit of the golfer and general amenity at the beach.

The invaluable strip of ground which Playfair was instrumental in reclaiming meant that a double width of fairway down the side of the beach became available. Following it a completely new first green was possible just across the Swilcan — and with it the right-hand course.

Some bunkers which had been logical traps for the left-hand course became redundant in the new plan, and a number were filled in. For the right-hand circuit new hazards were made, notably at the 5th and 6th fairways, to catch sliced balls. Some of the original left-hand bunkers survive. They are generally unnoticed because they are out of the path of most golfers unless they become unusually wayward. Near the tee of the 12th hole for instance, the bunker designed to trap approaches to the old High Hole, only penalises a badly topped drive scuttling from that tee or a long one, pulled badly, from the 7th tee. In the early days, Hill, Strath and the Shelly Bunkers were all in the direct line of the High Hole which was something of a terror, with the Eden as an additional hazard. Golfers have been known to play for years and then one day find themselves in a trap hitherto 'foreign terrain' to them, relics of the left-hand circuit.

The name of Tom Morris is closely associated with these revolutionary changes as they took place in the early years after his appointment in 1865 as greenkeeper. The work was carried out under his supervision, and in fact, in places by his own hand. Tom's careful custodianship in this way was in line with his reply to the golfers who deplored the stern taboo on Sunday golf that "the Links needed a rest if the golfers didn't."

One of the first jobs undertaken by him was the laying-down of a new last green. The original finishing hole was situated farther west, behind the little depression known as the Valley of Sin, that leads up to the present green. The area there was a large depression. This was filled up to the height of the raised plateau, to form the familiar, sloping Home Green.

Andra Kirkaldy records that his father was a labourer on the work of laying the new green. In the course of the work, as happens quite frequently in an old city like St. Andrews, human bones were exhumed.

One day Andra afterwards was standing with W. T. Linskill, a keen archaeologist as well as golfer, watching a big match finish. One of the players sent up a beautiful approach that made his putt a formality. Turning to Linskill, Andra chuckled:

> "You an' me kens there's mair than ba's lying dead on this green."

Interesting to recall now that, in 1896, soon after the New Course had been completed the Green Committee took an unprecedented course of action. In order to complete certain repair work on the Old and New Courses, they closed the first eight holes of the New in November, and the 10th and the two short holes of the Old, and substituted one wide, circular course. This was played for a week or two, Later, the 7th green of the Old Course was completely re-turfed. A shelter was constructed near it, and another at the Fifth Hole . . . the first concession to the occasionally rugged weather that can transform St. Andrews within minutes. For a time there were thoughts to make the circular course a permanency, but other counsels prevailed. But the potentiality is there, should the future dictate the need.

So, the Old Course remains today, its ancient turf as green and fresh as when golf began, despite the myriad feet that have trodden the same magic path, out and in again, throughout the centuries that stretch back into the mists of time. The historic Home of Golf.

> And still St. Andrews Links with
>   flags unfurl'd
> Shall peerless reign, and
>   challenge all the world!
>
>   (*George Fullerton Carnegie,* 1813)

HOW TO MASTER THE 'OLD'

THE standard length of the course is 6,566 yards, but for successive championships it has been lengthened. For the 1984 Championship it would be somewhere in the region of 6,936 yards. The Standard Scratch Score is 72. Until 1984 the course record was held by Neil Coles. In the first round of the 1970 Open, he scored 65. His card read:

Out: 4, 4, 4, 4, 4, 3, 2, 2, 4—31 65
In: 4, 3, 4, 4, 4, 4, 3, 4, 4—34

The general rule for playing the Old Course is to keep to the left off the tees. A player may hook with a fair degree of impunity, but it must be borne in mind that "the line to the left" often means a very difficult shot to the green.

370 Yards (374). 1st or BURN HOLE. Direction — Due West.

Par 4.

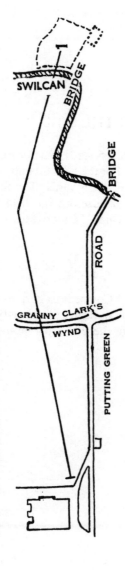

A public road crosses the line about 150 yards from the tee. The ground beyond the fence running along the north side of the fairway, including the footpath and the putting greens, is out of bounds. The Swilcan Burn guards the green. Shots trapped in the Burn can be lifted and dropped as near as possible to the place where the ball entered, but on the side furthest from the hole. Penalty, one stroke.

THE LINE to the hole is slightly to the left of the flag.

The Burn may frighten a timid player, but there is plenty of room behind, with nothing in the way of trouble, and the bold shot usually pays.

The short driver should play his second shot so as to be just short of the Burn, to be followed by an easy chip to the green.

411 Yards (411). 2nd, or DYKE HOLE. Direction — North-West.

Par 4.

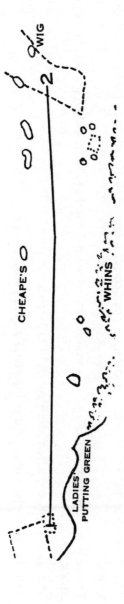

On the right there is rough with several bunkers all the way to the hole. Other bunkers are placed on the left-hand side, the principal one being Cheape's Bunker, with two others a little further on. Two bunkers to the left of the green, one just short, and the other beyond, demand careful placing. The green itself lies in a hollow, the ground in front and behind being higher.

THE LINE from the tee is to the right of Cheape's Bunker, and then straight to the hole.

The short driver should play his second to the right of the green, leaving a simple chip up for the third shot.

352 Yards (405). 3rd, or CARTGATE HOLE (Out). Direction—North-West by North. Par 4.

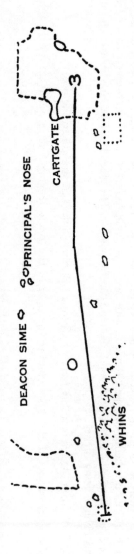

DEACON SIME ◇   ◇◇PRINCIPAL'S NOSE

CARTGATE

WHINS

There is rough to the right, through which passes a cart-track. A succession of three small bunkers is just clear of the rough.

On the left side is the Principal's Nose, a group of three bunkers near the railway, and on the edge of the green, Cartgate Bunker.

The green slopes away from the player with high ground in front.

THE LINE is a little to the right of the bunker which faces the tee.

419 Yards (470). 4th, or GINGER BEER HOLE. Direction – North-West by North.

Par 4.

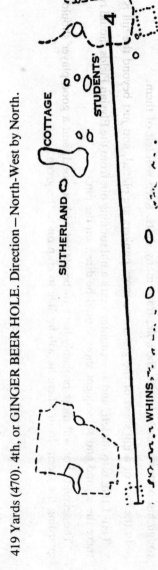

There are no hazards in the direct line to the hole, but two bunkers lie on the edge of the rough on the right, and two others on the same side near the green. The only other trouble that need be feared is the Students' Bunkers on the left near the green, and the bunkers at the side of and behind the flag. A feature of the hole is the little hump in front of the green.

TWO LINES may be taken. Straight on the pin all the way; or drive to the left for the plateau whose right fringe stops many straight shots. The green should be easily reached in two with an iron, but short drivers will probably require a wood, and may still be short. They should keep to the right of the flag.

514 Yards (567). 5th, or HOLE O' CROSS. Direction — North-West.

Par 5.

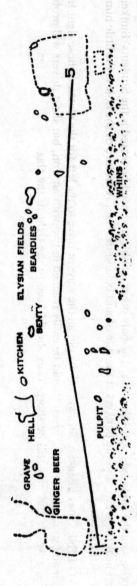

Beware the rough on the right. About 250 yards from the tee a group of seven bunkers, just at the edge of the rough but on the straight line to the hole, traps many shots. Keep well left of them.

In the face of a hill short of the green two more bunkers are placed, and just beyond the hill is a deep gully.

THE LINE is to the left, and as an aiming mark a hill running out from the Elysian Fields should be taken. From there the second and subsequent shots should be direct on the pin.

The second shot will most probably have to be played with a wood, and a good player should reach the hill guarding the green, from where he will be able to chip on to the green.

374 Yards (414). 6th, or HEATHERY HOLE (Out). Direction — North-West.   Par 4.

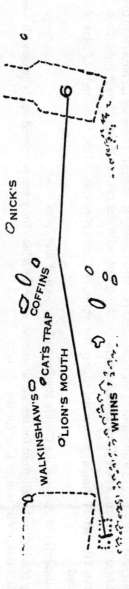

There are deep gullies to carry in front of the tee, and the hole is almost hidden from the tee by whins which line the right-hand side of the course. Several bunkers are interspersed about both sides of the fairway.

THE LINE to play is straight on the airfield hangars seen across the River Eden.

In front of the green, a rise hides a dip in the ground, and from the far side the putting surface slopes down to the back of the green. A shot pitched on the face of the rise and allowed to run should not be far from the flag.

359 Yards (364). 7th, or HIGH HOLE (Out). Direction — North-West then North.

Par 4.

This hole is dog-legged with whins to the right, until the 11th fairway is reached. There are no bunkers in the line until near the green, where Cockle Bunker is in the direct line, with the famous Strath Bunker quite close.

THE TEE SHOT should cut over the edge of the whins, and be so played as to land to the right of a big hill seen in front.

If doubtful of carrying the Cockle Bunker with the second shot, play short.

By playing to the left from the tee, an alternative route, by which the green is opened up, is given with a longer but less dangerous shot to play for the second.

166 Yards (163). 8th, or SHORT HOLE. Direction — East-South-East.

Par 3.

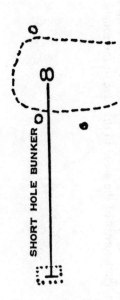

The ground from the tee to the green is rather broken up with little hollows.

Just in front of the green, and often in a direct line with the hole, is a little hill with a small and fairly deep bunker in the face. The ground in front and to the right of the bunker falls away, and as a result balls naturally run towards the bunker.

There is another bunker well to the right, but it should be easily avoided.

THE LINE is straight on the flag if the player is sure of reaching the green, but if not, a line on the highest church steeple should be taken. This will keep the player clear of the bunker should his shot be short.

307 Yards (359). 9th, or END HOLE. Direction — South-East.

Par 4.

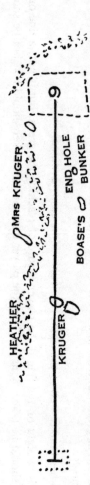

The ground in front of the tee is rough and broken. Twin bunkers, Kruger, are in the direct line about 100 yards from the tee, and to the left, among the heather, is Mrs Kruger.

Down the fairway, and slightly to the right, are two small bunkers, Boase's and the End Hole bunkers. Another bunker is situated at the near left-hand corner of the green in the edge of the rough.

THE LINE is straight on the flag.

318 Yards (338), 10th or BOBBY JONES HOLE. Direction — North-West.   Par. 4.

A group of bunkers menace the edge of the rough about 100 yards from the tee. Just to the right of the line about the length of a long drive, is another bunker, which catches many a slightly sliced drive. This hole was named 'BOBBY JONES' in 1972 in honour of the great golfer.

The green lies higher than the fairway, and slopes back.

THE TEE SHOT should be played just inside the line of the right-hand bunker.

172 Yards (170). 11th, or HIGH HOLE (In). Direction—West.   Par 3.

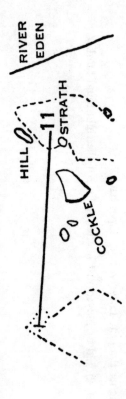

This famous green looks inviting, lying on a slope facing the tee, but is flanked on the left by Hill Bunker, a trap about 10 feet deep, and on the right by Strath Bunker, with Cockle Bunker on the right front. Over the back of the green is the bank of the River Eden, with rough, tufty grass.

A HOLE which can be played half a dozen ways in one week, depending on the strength and direction of the wind. An iron should be enough under normal conditions, to reach the green.

The difficulty with a stroke which goes over the back, is getting the ball to remain on the green on the return, particularly if the wind is blowing from the west.

316 Yards (360). 12th, or HEATHERY HOLE (In). Direction—South-East.

Par 4.

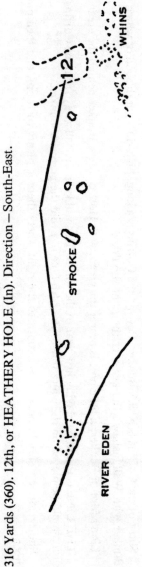

All bunkers to this hole are concealed from the tee.

There is a big deep one not far in front of the tee, with another big one, Stroke Bunker, about 170 yards away. Two smaller ones are situated a little further on, with another in a small hill in front of the green, which is long but very narrow.

THE LINE to the hole is well to the left on to the high heather-covered hill. This gives the best chance of a pitch that will hold the green. Alternatively, drive well to the right, but the approach is tighter.

398 Yards (427). 13th, or HOLE O' CROSS (In). Direction — South-East.

Par 4.

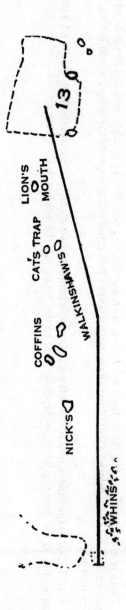

The Coffin Bunkers lie about the length of a good drive from the tee, slightly to the left.

Short of the Coffins is Nick's Bunker. Beyond the Coffins is a long, high ridge, at the end of which is Cat's Trap Bunker with Walkinshaw's Bunker over the right shoulder.

Lion's Mouth Bunker, a little pot, is nearer the green, with Hole o' Cross Bunker behind the green.

THE LINE is found by playing just clear of the whins. This will keep the ball away from the Coffins. The second shot should be played on the white flag of the fifth hole to avoid the greenside bunker.

Shorter drivers should play their seconds to the right where there is plenty of room, and then pitch on to the green.

523 Yards (560). 14th, or LONG HOLE (In). Direction — South-East.

Par 5.

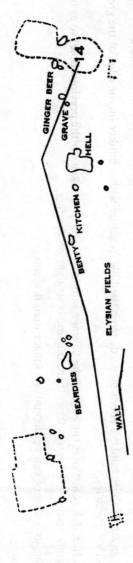

All ground to the right of the wall is out of bounds.

The first bunkers are the Beardies, a group of four, one big and deep, and the other three small. Benty Bunker comes next, followed by the Kitchen and Hell. Nearer the green are two small bunkers with Ginger Beer Bunker to the left.

THE CHURCH SPIRE to the right of the town is the line from the tee. Then play well off to the left on the square tower for the second, from there back to the right of the green.

The tee shot should get past the Beardies, between them and the wall, on the inviting Elysian Fields. The second shot, a brassie, should be well to the left of Hell Bunker. The green is raised above the level of the fairway and slopes down to the back.

401 Yards (413). 15th, or CARTGATE HOLE (In). Direction — South-East by South.

Par 4.

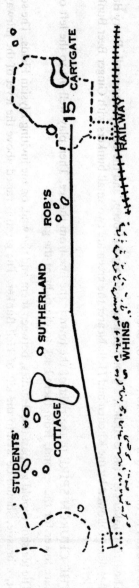

The Cottage Bunker lies about 150 yards from the tee, with Sutherland, a little pot, beyond it.

A group of three bunkers about 90 yards from the hole, together with a bunker on the edge of the green, form the other obstacles.

THE LINE is just over the edge of the Cottage Bunker (on the spire taken for the previous hole) so as to get into the gully seen from the tee; from there the line is straight on the flag.

The second shot can be deceptive — longer than it seems.

351 Yards (380). 16th, or CORNER OF THE DYKE HOLE. Direction — South-East by South. Par 4.

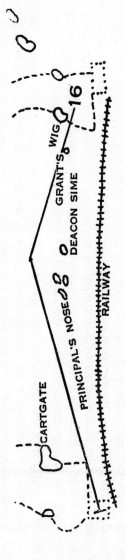

The railway fence bounds the fairway on the right, and is out of bounds. The Eden Course across the railway fence is out of bounds also.

About 180 yards from the tee is a group of bunkers, the Principal's Nose, with Deacon Sime just beyond. Near the green is Grant's Bunker, with Wig Bunker cutting into the green.

THE LINE to take is to the left of the Principal's Nose (between the two tall chimneys), playing back towards the right with the second shot; but some prefer to take the narrow line between the Principal's Nose and the railway fence.

461 Yards (466). 17th, or ROAD HOLE. Direction—South-East.

Par 5.

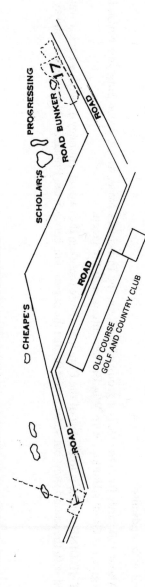

CHEAPE'S

SCHOLAR'S PROGRESSING

ROAD BUNKER 17

ROAD

ROAD

ROAD

OLD COURSE
GOLF AND COUNTRY CLUB

The Old Course Golf and Country Club on the right makes this a testing dog-legged hole. Opposite the corner of the boundary wall is Cheape's Bunker; then the player is clear of bunkers until near the green where the Scholar's Bunker and Progressing Bunker lie side by side. Behind the green is the notorious Road while the Road Bunker eats into the near side of the green. Only players who can guarantee a long carry should attempt to cut the corner over the Country Club. But having accomplished this, the player is left with a fair shot to the green.

FOR THE MAJORITY the drive should be played to the left. For the second shot, play to the right of the fairway, the ideal shot being up in the angle between the rough and the road, where a chip on to a long green is offered. It is dangerous to go for the green with a long shot, for the pitch back from the road is a gamble.

356 Yards (358). 18th, or TOM MORRIS HOLE. Direction — Due East.

Par 4.

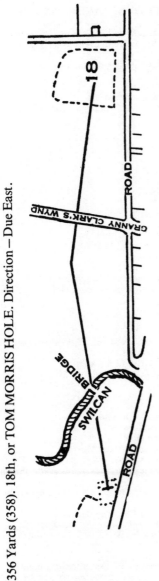

The only one obstacle to overcome is the Swilcan Burn which winds across the course less than 100 yards from the tee. The roadway, bounded by a fence continuing from the 18th green, is out of bounds. In front of the green is a deep hollow, the Valley of Sin, and the green itself lies sloping down from the back right-hand corner.

THE LINE to the hole is on the clock of the R. and A. Clubhouse.

On the green remember the slope, as it is more pronounced than it looks. The green is usually the stiffest on the course.

HISTORICAL DATES IN STORY OF ST. ANDREWS GOLF

1457 Golf forbidden by Act of Scots Parliament, and archery practice demanded.
1553 Archbiship John Hamilton confirms St. Andrews townspeople's rights to play golf over Links.
1598 Town Church complaint of congregation golfing during hours of service.
1618 First ball improvement—the "featherie".
1629 Marquis of Montrose golfing at St. Andrews.
1691 St. Andrews described as the "Metropolis of Golfing".
1754 Society of St. Andrews Golfers founded in St. Andrews because it is the "Alma Mater of Golf".
1759 First reference to stroke play in Rules.
1764 First introduction of 18 holes.
1777 First rules for tee-ing.
1787 First stymie rule.
1797 Town Council sells Links.
1805 "Rabbits" Lawsuit over Links.
1806 Society of Golfers make captaincy elective.
1812 First revision of original rules of 1744.
1817 St. Andrews Thistle Club, first tradesmen's Club, founded.
1821 First survey of Old Course.
1832 Greens doubled in size to speed up play.
1834 Society of Golfers became "Royal and Ancient Golf Club".
1836 Longest featherie drive recorded—361 yards.
1838 First rule for lost ball penalty.
1843 St. Andrews Golf Club founded under name of Mechanics Club.
1845 Proposed railway threatens to cut through Links at Burn Hole. R. and A. successful in having it re-routed.
1848 First Gutta Ball on market.
1851 Railway line built alongside Links.
1854 R. and A. Clubhouse built.
1855 Institution of two greens at the High Hole. New rules include provision for lifting a ball off sheets being washed or dried.
1857 First-ever championship, a foursomes event, at St. Andrews.
1858 Allan Robertson first professional and first man to break 80.
1858 First steward at golf match.
1859 Death of Allan Robertson.
1860 First Open Championship.
1865 Tom Morris appointed first professional of R. and A.
1867 First-ever Ladies' Club formed at St. Andrews.
1868 Protecting fence put around new Home Hole.
1869 Patent Hole-Cutter invented and presented to Tom Morris.
1870 "Young Tom" wins third successive Open. New first green laid down.
1872 New Trophy awarded and won by Young Tom, making his fourth title in a row.
1873 First deliberately ribbed club used in the Open by Tom Kidd. First Open played at St. Andrews.
1874 Fence erected to separate Links from road following legal decision preventing Town Council from taking part of Links for building.
1875 Death of Young Tom at age of 24 years. W. T. Linskill, St. Andrews, forms Cambridge University Golfing Society.
1876 R. and A. and Union Club amalgamate.
1877 First notices to "Replace Turf", also erection of special teeing grounds.
1885 R. and A. approached to form an Association under one set of rules.

1881   First passing of rule: loss of hole for driving out of bounds.
1886   Only year left-handed course used in a championship.
1888   R. and A. issue Rules of Golf to all golf clubs.
1890   First canvas golf club container used.
1892   Freddie Tait's record drive.
1893   Willie Auchterlonie wins Open. Peter Anderson wins Amateur.
1894   Town regains possession of Links. New Parliamentary Order sets out arrangements with R. and A.
1894   Winner of Open receives £40.
1895   New Course opened.
1897   R. and A. given sole control of Rules of Golf Committee.
1900   Death of Freddie Tait in South Africa.
1902   Sandy Herd uses Haskell Rubber Ball to win Open. New Golf Club founded.
1908   Death of Tom Morris.
1913   First charge for golf levied on visitors.
1914   Eden Course opened.
1919   R. and A. take over management of British Championships.
1921   St. Andrews-born Jock Hutchison wins Open and takes trophy across Atlantic for first time.
1922   Prince of Wales plays in as Captain of R. and A.
1929   R. and A. legalise steel shafts in this country.
1930   Duke of York plays in as Captain. Bobby Jones wins Amateur on Old Course as part of his "Grand Slam".
1933   First charge of gate money on spectators.
1936   Bobby Jones' nostalgic round.
1938   First victory in Walker Cup.
1946   End of free golf in St. Andrews. Introduction of crowd control for matches.
1950   First Commonwealth Tournament played. Australia wins.
1951   Four-day Conference of Britain, Dominion and U.S. Association on unifying Rules. Stymie abolished. First American Captain of R. and A. elected, Mr Francis Ouimet.
1953   Joint Links Committee formed.
1955   First Open televised.
1958   First Eisenhower Trophy played on Old Course. Freedom of St. Andrews presented to Bobby Jones.
1959   First Ladies' Commonwealth Team Tourney on Old Course.
1960   Centenary Open Championship at·St. Andrews.
1961   First all-TV matches in Britain on Old Course.
1966   First colour TV Challenge Match (Gleneagles, Carnoustie, St. Andrews) in Britain.
1967   First Sunday play allowed for Alcan Tourney and future Open replays.
1967   Alcan World Championship, world's biggest money tournament, inaugurated on Old Course.
1968   Laurie Auchterlonie Golf Museum opened. Old Course Hotel opened. World Amateur Senior Team Championship. St. Andrews Golf Club's 125th anniversary.
1969   Traffic lights installed on 1st and 18th fairways. Wheatley Report issued. St. Andrews to Leuchars railway line closed.
1970   Open Championship—Sunday practice allowed. Jack Nicklaus wins after play-off with Doug Sanders.
1971   Ground at Balgove purchased for beginners' course. Second British Walker Cup win. Death of Bobby Jones.
1972   Bing Crosby Tournament inaugurated. Tenth Hole dedicated to Bobby Jones. Zenya Hamada Trust formed. Balgove course opened.
1973   Scottish Ladies' Championship. Sunbeam Electric Scottish Open Championship.
1974   St. Andrews Links Order Confirmation Act received the Royal Assent: Links Trust and Links Management Committee formed.
1975   Joseph C. Dey, Second American Captain of R. and A. plays himself into office.

1976   Great Britain and Ireland beat Europe for St. Andrews Trophy.
1977   L.G.U. Headquarters move to St. Andrews. Death of Jock Hutchison in United States.
1978   Fairway watering installed on Old Course. Open Championship — Jack Nicklaus wins.
1979   Colgate Match Play Championship — Vicente Fernandez wins.
1980   Rusack's Hotel sold to Links Trust.
1981   Death of A. O. Cheape, Laird of Strathtyrum.
1982   Mr Frank Sheridan buys Old Course Hotel.
1983   Old Course Golf and Country Club formally opened by HRH The Princess Anne. Links Changing Rooms Complex opened in lower ground floor of Rusack's Hotel.
1984   Open Championship.

INDEX